WITHDRAWAL

QUALITATIVE INQUIRY THROUGH A CRITICAL LENS

This volume highlights work being done in qualitative inquiry through a variety of critical lenses such as new materialism, queer theory, and narrative inquiry. Contributors ranging from seasoned academics to emerging scholars attend to questions of ontology and epistemology, providing, in the process, insights that any qualitative researcher interested in the state of the field would find of value. The authors

- rethink taken-for-granted paradigms, frameworks, methodologies, ethics, and politics;
- demonstrate major shifts in qualitative inquiry and point readers in new and exciting directions;
- advocate for a critical qualitative inquiry that addresses social justice, decolonization, and the politics of research;
- present plenary addresses and other key original papers from the 2015 International Congress of Qualitative Inquiry.

This title is sponsored by the International Association of Qualitative Inquiry, a major new international organization that sponsors an annual Congress.

Norman K. Denzin is Distinguished Professor of Communications, College of Communications Scholar, and Research Professor of Communications, Sociology, and Humanities at the University of Illinois, Urbana–Champaign.

Michael D. Giardina is Associate Professor of Sport, Culture, and Politics and Associate Director of the Center for Sport, Health, and Equitable Development at Florida State University.

QUALITATIVE INQUIRY THROUGH A CRITICAL LENS

*Edited by Norman K. Denzin
and Michael D. Giardina*

Routledge
Taylor & Francis Group

NEW YORK AND LONDON

First published 2016
by Routledge
711 Third Avenue, New York, NY 10017

and by Routledge
2 Park Square, Milton Park, Abingdon, Oxon, OX14 4RN

Routledge is an imprint of the Taylor & Francis Group, an informa business

© 2016 Taylor & Francis

The right of the editors to be identified as the authors of the editorial material, and of the authors for their individual chapters, has been asserted in accordance with sections 77 and 78 of the Copyright, Designs and Patents Act 1988.

Trademark notice: Product or corporate names may be trademarks or registered trademarks, and are used only for identification and explanation without intent to infringe.

Library of Congress Cataloging-in-Publication Data
A catalog record has been requested.

ISBN: 978-1-62958-501-7 (hbk)
ISBN: 978-1-62958-502-4 (pbk)
ISBN: 978-1-315-54594-3 (ebk)

Typeset in Bembo
by Apex CoVantage, LLC

CONTENTS

ACKNOWLEDGMENTS

We thank the publisher of all publishers, Mitch Allen, for his unwavering support and guidance over our ten-year relationship with Left Coast Press; his commitment to qualitative inquiry is unsurpassed. We extend our sincere appreciation to the entire Left Coast Press staff with whom we have worked over the years, especially Ryan Harris, Stephanie Adams, Michael Jennings, and Hannah Jennings for their contributions. We also thank Catherine Bernard at Routledge for making the transition to our new publishing home as smooth as possible; we look forward to working with her and her staff in the coming years. Thanks are also due to Sheri Sipka for managing the production of the volume, as well as to Neal Ternes for assistance in gathering the index. Many of the chapters contained in this book were presented as plenary or keynote addresses at the Eleventh International Congress of Qualitative Inquiry, held at the University of Illinois, Urbana–Champaign, in May 2015. We thank the Institute of Communications Research, the College of Media, and the International Institute for Qualitative Inquiry for continued support of the Congress as well as those campus units that contributed time, fund, and/or volunteers to the effort.

The Congress, and by extension this book, would not have materialized without the tireless efforts of Mary Blair, Katia Curbelo, Bryce Henson, Robin Price, Nathalie Tiberghien, and James Salvo (the glue who continues to hold the whole thing together).

For information on future Congresses, please visit http://www.icqi.org.

Norman K. Denzin
Michael D. Giardina
December 2015

INTRODUCTION

Qualitative Inquiry Through a Critical Lens

Norman K. Denzin and Michael D. Giardina

> Maybe I'm just out of step with the world, but what some of us are fighting for is the principle that not everything that is valuable can or should be monetized. That universities are one of the custodians of centuries of knowledge, curiosity, inspiration. That education is not a commodity; it's a qualitative transformation. You can't sell it. You can't simply transfer it.
>
> —Sarah Churchwell, 2015

Proem

On December 15, 2015, J. Bruce Harreld, president of the University of Iowa, issued an apology for stating at a December 9 meeting of the University of Iowa Staff Council that any instructor who began class without having completed a lesson plan, or who was otherwise unprepared to teach his or her class that day, "should be shot" (quoted in Woodhouse, 2015). Coming on the heels of numerous school shootings over the last decade, ranging from the massacres at Sandy Hook Elementary School in 2012 (26 dead) and Virginia Tech University in 2007 (32 dead) to the *four(!)* university shootings that took place between October and November of 2015 alone—as well as the increasingly political nature of gun violence in the United States, which has resulted in widespread calls for universities to allow faculty and students alike to carry guns on campus (see Fernandez & Montgomery, 2015)—Harreld's remarks shed renewed light on the fact that the newly installed president had come to his job not from the typical ranks of academia (e.g., as a dean, provost, chancellor, etc.) but from industry with large-scale companies where he had previously served in numerous leadership positions at Kraft General Foods, Boston Market Company, and IBM.

At issue here is not Harreld's specific remarks, ridiculous and offensive though they are. Rather, the remarks make us question how a former mid-level executive from IBM with no experience in higher education other than several adjunct business faculty appointments over the years ascended to the presidency of a major research university in the first place—a position that many faculty at the university believe he was unqualified to hold in the first place (see Woodhouse, 2015). Ed Wasserman (2015), former president of the University of Iowa Faculty Senate, maintained in the *Iowa City Press-Citizen* that, although the university publicly interviewed four candidates (three of whom held senior administrative positions in academia), a Freedom of Information Act request revealed that while Parker Executive Search "authenticated the credentials, passed along the completed dossiers to the official search and screen committee, and contacted references" (para. 2), the president of the Board of Regents, Bruce Rastetter, was simultaneously arranging for private meetings with handpicked candidates of his own, including Harreld, who met with five regents several weeks before his formal campus interview; Harreld also received a personal phone call from Iowa governor Terry Branstad (Charis-Carlson, 2015). Despite the other three strong academic candidates, it was Harreld who was unanimously chosen by the Board of Regents as the new president, even though his public presentation was widely panned as weak and unprofessional (including a moment in which Harreld claimed he had only used Wikipedia to gain information about the university prior to his interview) and though surveys showed he had almost no support among faculty or students.

This abdication of higher education to the nexus of politics and corporate fealty is not an isolated case. Nor is it, we would add, the worst case we have seen in the last year. That honor would go to the public circus that was the forced resignation of popular University of North Carolina–system president, Tom Ross, in January 2015 (Carpenter, 2015). The well-credentialed Ross—who was formerly a judge, president of Davidson College, chairman of the University of North Carolina–Greensboro Board of Trustees, and executive director of the Z. Smith Reynolds Foundation—was by all accounts respected by students and faculty and considered to be doing a fine job. Despite his successes, however, the UNC Board of Governors decided to move in another direction, one largely influenced by the sharp rightward shift in politics within the state that had led to the gubernatorial election of a Republican, Pat McCrory, in 2013 (Purdy, 2015), who had famously said during a radio interview that the state shouldn't subsidize courses in "gender studies or Swahili," and who endeavored to "reform and adapt the UNC brand to the ever-changing competitive environment of the twenty-first century" by "honing in on skills and subjects employers need" (quoted in Purdy, 2015).

It was in this context that the replacement for Ross, and the conditions under which he was forced out of his position, became publicly contentious. We should note as well that higher education in North Carolina is an especially political beast. Prior to Ross, the UNC-system president was Erskine Bowles, who was White House chief of staff for U.S. president Bill Clinton from 1997–1998 and who ran unsuccessfully for U.S. Senate in North Carolina twice; he currently sits on numerous corporate boards, including General Motors and Facebook. Bowles was also appointed to his position with some degree of controversy; namely, public hearings on his candidacy were never held. To this end, it was not entirely surprising when the Republican-dominated UNC Board of Governors selected Margaret Spellings, a former U.S. secretary of education under President George W. Bush, as the new UNC-system president. Spellings, a Republican political operator who was head of the George W. Bush Presidential Center in Dallas at the time of her appointment, also served Bush as the political director for his 1994 gubernatorial campaign and later as a senior adviser during his tenure as governor of Texas.

For her part, Spellings was transparent in addressing what many observers viewed was a *political* appointment, because it most certainly *was* a political appointment. She stated in part:

> You know, these are all political settings. That's how we make public policy in this setting and in this state. . . . So you bet, I think it's a fantastic way to make policy, is in a political setting.
>
> *(quoted in Strauss, 2015, para. 8)*

The result of this political choice is a university-system president who openly refers to students as "customers," who sees for-profit higher education as a positive force (she has served on the board of the University of Phoenix's parent company, the Apollo Group), and who has come under fire for repeatedly making homophobic remarks (see Carpenter, 2015). She was one of the principle proponents of No Child Left Behind and, as secretary of education, "convened the Commission on the Future of Higher Education, which in 2006 released a report with controversial recommendations, including a call for colleges and universities to focus on training students for the workforce and supporting research with commercial applications" (Strauss, 2015, para. 6). This history does not a positive picture of her tenure paint.

Yet these kinds of policy decisions and political appointments are the new normal in which we are located, a historical present that has seen political expediency and partisanship forcefully co-opt the spaces of higher education, one that is increasingly devoid of any orientation other than to that of the free market. In a previous book (see Denzin & Giardina, 2015a), we unpacked the commercial interests governing the corporate university of today, one marked not only by the influx of brand signifiers on university campuses, buildings, and research parks (e.g., McDonalds, Starbucks, AT&T, Google, etc.) and student entertainment centers (e.g., the $64.5 million 'lazy river' swimming pool in the shape of the Louisiana State University logo at its remolded fitness center) but by the commodification of knowledge, the marketization of science, and the bureaucratic managerialism of faculty. To this we add the overt and explicit politicizing of the university itself (acknowledging, of course, that it has always been a site of political struggle), a moment in which appointing a political figure or businessperson is simply the logical outcome of treating it like an extension of the legislature or governor's office or as a business concern that can yield a positive return on investment for the state.

We see this notion not only in calls for 'special' consideration to be given to STEM fields (*Science, Technology, Engineering,* and *Math*) due to their perceived benefit to the job market but in the overt way that curricular design and university governance have increasingly become the purview of state legislators and other local and national politicians, as well as big money donors and right-wing pundits (e.g., the Salaita case at the University of Illinois; drastic funding cuts to the University of Wisconsin system; universities virtually extorting students to subsidize athletics programs or build new stadiums via exorbitant student fees; etc.). In the most extreme of these situations, we also see individuals appointed to state legislative committees overseeing education who are anti-intellectual and anti-science, such as when Andy Biggs, Senate president in Arizona, named State Senator Sylvia Allen chairwoman of the Arizona Senate Education Committee, who in her role "will control which legislative education proposals succeed and which ones die" (Rau, 2015, para. 6). Allen, who did not attend college, has gone on record as stating her belief that Earth is only 6,000 years old, made Facebook posts endorsing bizarre conspiracy theories, and has openly suggested "mandatory church attendance" (ibid., para. 3).[1]

This order of things is not restricted to the United States, of course. Recently in Japan, 26 of the 60 national universities that offer courses in social sciences and the humanities "have confirmed that they will either close or scale back their relevant faculties at the behest of Japan's government," which called on them to take "active steps to abolish [social science and humanities] organizations or to convert them to serve areas that better meet society's needs" (Grove, 2015, para. 2–3). Unsurprisingly, these 'needs' are those found in STEM fields, according to the minister of education. In Australia, too, the Abbot government in 2013 promised to shift $93.6 million from research in the humanities into scientific medical research, in the process singling out "increasingly ridiculous" research grants in the humanities as one reason for the shift (Delaney, 2013). Similarly, as Marina Warner (2015) explains regarding the current state of higher education in the United Kingdom, "Cuts [to the budget] are the tools of the ideological decision to stop subsidizing tuition and to start withdrawing from directly supporting research. What we are in effect moving towards is the privatization of higher education ... [as] universities are beaten into the shapes dictated by business" (para. 7, 15).

As a form of governance, argues Henry Giroux (2014), this "current assault threatening higher education and the humanities in particular cannot be understood outside of the crisis of economics, politics, and power"—a crisis that reveals itself in the "increasing pace of the corporatization and militarization of the university, the squelching of academic freedom, the rise of an ever increasing contingent of part-time faculty, the rise of a bloated managerial class, and the view that students are basically consumers and faculty providers of a saleable commodity such as a credential or a set of workplace skills" (p. 16). In this way, and following Wendy Brown (2015), it might behoove us to view our neoliberal present not as a form of economic policy but rather as "a peculiar form of reason," one that is "converting the distinctly political character, meaning, and operation of democracy's constituent elements into economic ones" (p. 17). In practical terms, we see this in operation with the preeminence given to university athletic, marketing, and promotion department budgets; the privileging of entrepreneurial programs and centers,[2] STEM education, and massive open online courses (MOOCs); the often zealous emphasis placed on procuring external grant funding (and the correlative emphasis on faculty hires who can work within such—usually positivist—spaces); the marketization of science and knowledge; and the stifling of public intellectualism within a faculty cowed by assaults on extramural political speech, activism, and the humanistic education of young people.

All of the above, we submit, have, either implicitly or explicitly, an impact on the *research act*—on the way qualitative inquiry and critical scholarship is shaped, constrained, contested, funded, and taught in such environments. *It is against this collective tide that we swim, seeking a critical, qualitative inquiry, a critical global community of scholars, a new social awakening—an academy that pushes back.*

Through a Critical Lens[3]

In our work on qualitative inquiry (see, e.g., Denzin, 2009, 2010; Denzin & Giardina, 2006; 2008; 2012; 2015a; 2015b; Giardina & Laurendeau, 2013; Giardina & Newman, 2014), we have repeatedly made the case that questions of evidence, knowledge, and research practice are inherently intertwined with the changing face of the university—with the changing face of higher education itself—in all of its various social, cultural, political, and economic forms. What our historical present suggests, we argue, is that those in higher education—especially those scholars in the humanities and social sciences doing critical, feminist, poststructural, postmodern, and posthuman research—face a crossroads, one in which (a) the act of research is inherently political; (b) that act is governed by a particular free-market politics of research in the corporate university; (c) (post-)positivism still dominates this conversation; and (d) anti-foundational approaches to research are often marginalized or forced to sit alongside foundationalist perspectives in the problematic 'mixed methods' space. We have covered this ground before (see Denzin & Giardina, 2015b) and thus will not rehash it here. Suffice it to say, this is an ongoing point of contestation within and between the qualitative inquiry community (such that we can speak to a 'community' of qualitative researchers at all). Instead, we want to consider an alternative mode of thinking about the critical turn in qualitative inquiry and posit the following suggestion: *perhaps it is time we turned away from 'methodology' altogether.*

What does this mean? Writing in *Reconceptualizing Qualitative Research*, Mirka Koro-Ljungberg (2015) puts forward the idea of 'methodologies without methodology', which "represents methodologies without strict boundaries or normative structures—methodologies that may begin anywhere, anytime, but by doing so can create a sense of uncertainty and loss (or mourning of stable, fixed, preconceptualized, or historical knowledge.... They can begin anywhere, stay (at least temporarily) lost and uncertain, and still promote change in onto-epistemological practices" (p. 1).[4] Koro-Ljungberg's argument is grounded firmly in debates over *post*-qualitative research—especially those in relationship to new empiricism / new materialism. What she is suggesting, in part, is not that we should evacuate methodology *per se* from the act of research but rather that we might do well to get outside or beyond the idea that an approach to understanding a given topic (i.e., race, class, gender, sexuality, the body, globalization, etc.) should be *"formalized, precise, and methods-driven"* (St. Pierre, 2015, p. 75, our emphasis).

Drawing especially from Deleuze and Guattari, Elizabeth St. Pierre (2015) explains this notion further:

> [T]he very idea of method [*ED: within humanist qualitative research*] forces one into a prescribed order of thought and practices that prohibits the experimental nature of transcendental empiricism. Method proscribes and prohibits. It controls and disciplines. Further, method always comes too late, is immediately out-of-date and so inadequate to the task at hand. But method not only can't keep up with events, more seriously, it prevents them from coming into existence. One might say that "method," as we think of it in the methodological individualism of conventional humanist qualitative methodology with its methods of data collection and methods of data analysis, *cannot be thought or done in new empirical inquiry*. . . . In fact, the new empiricist might well argue that attempting to follow a given research method will likely foreclose possibilities for the "new." The new empiricist researcher, then, is on her own, inventing inquiry in the doing. Hence, we have methods-driven research that mostly repeats what is recognizable, *what is already known.*
>
> *(pp. 79, 81, second emphasis ours)*[5]

And we should not merely be repeating what is already known! Although this might not seem like a radical proposition for some, this is *not* how students are generally taught to think about research in the present moment. Rather, they are more often than not taught particular '*methods of data collection*' (such as interviews, case studies, focus groups, ethnography, other basic research design techniques, etc.) within the context of research methods or research design courses; it is few and far between that philosophy of science and philosophy of inquiry seminars are required of graduate students—and even fewer still, we would contend, that call into question or contest the very notion of data or evidence itself. Moreover, this next generation of researchers continues to be funneled into a professorial system in which the 'gold standard' remains so-called scientifically based research (in order to survive, many simply go along with the status quo or 'adapt' their research to better 'fit' within a dominant political orientation).

This has to stop.

In the last decade, there has been an explosion of literatures, theories, frameworks, and turns, from the affective turn (Gregg & Seigworth, 2010; Clough & Halley, 2007), to the new (feminist) materialisms and ontologies (Coole & Frost, 2010), to calls for post-methodological, post-humanist, post-empirical, and post-qualitative frameworks (Lather, 2007; Lather & St. Pierre, 2013; St. Pierre, 2013; MacLure, 2013; Jackson & Mazzei, 2012), to transnational queer indigenous studies (Driskill, Finley, Gilley, & Morgenson, 2011), to performative critical race theories (Alexander, 2012; Johnson, 2003), to new alignments between rhetoric and performance studies (Gencarella & Pezzullo, 2010; Fenske & Goltz, 2014), to a resurgence in the global community performance and applied theatre movements (Cohen-Cruz, 2010; Kuppers & Robertson, 2007; Madison, 2010). In these new spaces, theory turns back on itself, re-reading itself through the biographical, the historical, and the ideological. A re-born critical theory is imagined. Strategies and tactics of resistance against racism, sexism, homophobia, and a global geopolitical system out of control are called for. The affective turn resists the war machine, the corporate commodification of science and knowledge—untangling and re-doing nested relations of power, bodies, life, death, and desire (Garoian & Gaudelius, 2008; see also Agamben, 1998; Ahmed, 2006; Braidotti, 2013). And in each of these instances above, it is the work of *theory* that is the driving imperative; the work of theory and its intersection with—or perhaps revealing of—(new) critical methodologies.

Consider the following: a decade ago, the field of autoethnography was just gaining a foothold (Jones, Adams, & Ellis, 2013) and had yet to be linked with the performance turn in anthropology and communication studies (see, e.g., Schechner, 2013; Madison, 2010). Critical pedagogy was a literature unto itself, a branch of critical theory, with links to the Frankfurt School, Jürgen Habermas, Antonio Gramsci, Paulo Freire, and Augusto Boal. Influenced by a call to rhetorical reflexivity, which questions the writer's so-called objective place in the text, a new autoethnographic turn was taken (Conquergood, 1991; Geertz, 1988). This has produced a proliferation of new writing forms, including variations on performance writing from fiction, to poetry, to sociopoetics, to ethnodramas. Multiple forms of ethnography and autoethnography exist and are deployed in various ways—narrative, critical, collaborative, queer, quare, global, grounded, situational, performative, feminist, decolonizing, meta, co-constructed, duo, and so on (see, e.g., Norris, Sawyer, & Lund, 2012; Wyatt, Gale, Gannon, & Davies, 2011; Saldaña, 2011; Spry, 2011; Jones, Adams, & Ellis, 2015). All of these turns and writing forms place traditional concepts of performance, ethnography, narrative, meaning, voice, presence, and representation under contestation and erasure. Together they politicize the "interpretive, affective turn."

Within such turns, we should not lose sight of the *ontological orientations* through which research is conducted. Or, to put it differently, we might do well to consider what it would mean to think *onto-epistemologically* about the research act. Take the case of interviewing, a classic social scientific method for 'collecting' empirical material that is widely taught in introductory research methods courses and contained in numerous research methods textbooks. Lisa Mazzei (2013) offers that the interview is and has been fundamentally situated within humanist theories of the subject, which "typically equate words spoken by participants in interviews and then transcribed into words in interview transcripts as data … in which that voice is produced by a unique, essentialist subject" (p. 732). Many qualitative researchers would consider this position to be orthodoxy. She counters this view, however, by explaining how, within a *post-humanist* stance, "interview data, the voices of participants, cannot be thought as emanating from an essentialist subject nor can they be separated from the enactment in which they are produced, an enactment of researcher-data-participants-theory-analysis—what I call here a *Voice without Organs* (VwO)" (p. 732, emphasis in original). As Mazzei argues, theorizing the interview in such a way "requires different conceptions of human agency" (p. 733); from a humanist perspective, "agency is an innate characteristic of the essentialist, intentional free subject" (p. 733); from the poststructural perspective, agency "seems to lie in the subject's ability to decode and record its identity within discursive formations and cultural practices" (p. 733)—a politics of language and representation at work.

But from the post-humanist perspective, "agency is distributed in a way that avoids hanging on to the vestiges of a knowing humanist subject that lingers in some poststructural analysis . . . [such that] intentionality is not attributable to humans" (p. 733) but rather is, after Karen Barad (2007), "understood as attributable to a complex network of human and nonhuman agents, including historically specific sets of material conditions that exceed the traditional notion of the individual (p. 23; also cited in Mazzei, 2013, p. 734). The implication of thinking ontologically about the interview, then, as St. Pierre (2015) reminds us, is, "The onto-epistemological formation that celebrates the speech of the humanist human and assigns it pre-eminent value and practice application as scientific discourse is not the onto-epistemological formation of post-qualitative inquiry" (p. 80). For this reason, she continues,

> we should think, and should always have thought, twice before proposing research projects with, for example, an awkward combination of an interview study and a Foucaultian genealogy or a rhizo-analysis of interview data, projects that indicate *ontological confusion*.
>
> *(p. 80, emphasis ours)*

It is this last point—avoiding ontological confusion—that can only come from a deep engagement with the philosophy of inquiry, an understanding of epistemology and ontology and how they intersect in the research act—especially since the influx of post-methodologists, post-humanist, post-empirical, and post-qualitative frameworks call for *new* models of science, second empiricisms, reimagined social sciences, capacious sciences, sciences of *différance*, a science defined by becoming, a double(d) science (Lather, 2007; St. Pierre, 2013, p. 613; MacLure, 2011).[6]

As part of being open to the messy politics of our field(s), there needs to be a greater openness to alternative paradigm critique. We need to work through the beliefs that organize our interpretive communities, including our theories of being (ontology), knowing (epistemology), inquiry (methodology), moral conduct (ethics), praxis, politics, truth, voice, and representation (for a critique of these terms, see St. Pierre, 2011). It is insufficient to throw out the word "paradigm" because you don't like it (see Lincoln, 2010), especially since paradigm dominance often involves control of graduate curricula, recruitment funding, and faculty appointments.

Given the increasing disruptions to and splinterings within the field, we believe it is necessary to confront and work through the criticisms that continue to be directed to qualitative inquiry, from both inside and outside the field. Indeed, the chapters in this volume speak not with one homogenous voice but as a collection of diverse voices that take seriously the idea of disagreement and dissent. Thus, the reader will find chapters in this volume that at various turns agree, disagree, and conflict with each other, in the hopes that focusing a critical lens on the work of theory as it relates to the conduct of research will yield new and exciting possibilities.

The Chapters

Qualitative Inquiry Through a Critical Lens is loosely organized into three sections: "Theoretical Imperatives"; "Methodological Interventions"; and "Performing Inquiry." The volume begins with Elizabeth Adams St. Pierre's chapter ("The Long Reach of Logical Positivism / Logical Empiricism"), which provides a critical interrogation of how logical positivism / logical empiricism continues to influence the intersection of higher education policy, assumptions about 'science,' and the conduct of research. To do this, she reviews the epistemological project of empiricism and the knowledge generated therefrom, as well its connection to scientism. She then positions humanist qualitative methodology in response to logical positivism while also indicting it for never truly moving beyond a "methods-driven, objective approach" to the research act.

In chapter 2, Margaret Kovach ("Moving Forward, Pushing Back: Indigenous Methodologies in the Academy") draws attention to Indigenous methodologies and, correlatively, Indigenous knowledges, worldview, and communities through which they are grounded and enacted—an Indigenous ontology. To do so, she points to examples of Indigenous methodology being deployed successfully within the academy. Kovach then presents a particular set of guidelines for researchers who wish to engage in and with Indigenous methodology. She concludes her chapter by examining a recent research project she was involved with that focused on the experiences of faculty members—both Indigenous and not—who take up Indigenous knowledges in their classrooms, research, and academic life.

In chapter 3, Kathy Charmaz ("The Power of Stories and the Potential of Theorizing for Social Justice Studies") argues that although qualitative researchers have long demonstrated the power of stories—such as in telling stories about the lives of individuals, including our own—those stories have not always been fully theorized. She begins her chapter by reviewing critiques of interviews and interviewing as a strategy of inquiry. Next, she turns to grounded theory, reading it through (if not against) "epistemological questions and methodological innovations" that have occurred over the last few decades. She then discusses questions of "coding qualitative data" and the implications thereof, before exploring the use of grounded theory in social justice research.

In section 2, attention is turned to methodological interventions drawn from the poetry of interviews and documents, 'listening', and the queering and quaring of autoethnography. In chapter 4, Valerie Janesick ("Poetic Inquiry: Transforming Qualitative Data into Poetry") focuses on the use of poetry in research. She begins by providing a brief history of poetry in research. She then introduces the reader the concepts of 'found poetry' and 'identity poetry,' providing numerous examples of these strategies in action. She concludes by providing a roadmap for those wishing to begin engaging in such poetic practices.

In chapter 5, Bronwyn Davies ("Emergent Listening") explores the epistemology and ontology of selves "emergent in the space of listening," or what she calls "emergent listening." Drawing from the work of Jean-Luc Nancy, among others, Davies challenges us to view listening "as a multi-sensual encounter with the world," in which the self is not separate from the world but rather "a self emergent with/in the world, open to the world." To this end, she engages with Gilles Deleuze's understanding of 'difference,' Karen Barad's concept of 'diffraction,' and Henri Bergson's thinking about "lines of ascent and descent," inviting us to move beyond reflexivity. She then explores listening to children at play in a Swedish preschool and how doing so reveals the "ongoing rehearsal of the skills necessary to ensure recognition of themselves within those categories they have been assigned, enabling them to live out the identification of self within any number of binary stratifications, endlessly rehearsing the specificity of their positioning within the existing repetitive order."

In chapter 6, Robin M. Boylorn and Tony E. Adams "(Queer and Quare Autoethnography") explore how autoethnography can enhance queer and quare research. More specifically, they ask, Who can be queer and who can be quare? Which bodies are most at risk by trying to live queerly, or quarely, in social life? Writing their respective selves into and through the research act, Boylorn and Adams illustrate how autoethnography can both ground queer theory "in lived, concrete circumstances" and allow quare theory "to make better use of reflexivity and excel in its commitment to social justice."

In chapter 7 ("This Is Not a Collaborative Writing"), Mirka Koro-Ljungberg and Jasmine B. Ulmer challenge "humanistic and anthropocentric writings," noting, "in current virtual and nomadic worlds writing, writers, and collaboration takes different and unanticipated forms including anti- or post-human extensions." To this end, they wonder "how one can engage in collaborative writing if the words, ideas, images, or concepts are problematized and they belong to nobody or everybody all at once." This is the presence and absences of the 'new writing,' of collisions between Gilles Deleuze, Jacques Derrida, Michel Foucault, Roland Barthes, and others that challenges conventional humanist understandings of the world, of what writing is/does/can be/isn't at once and the same, starting from the middle of something being erased through its very acts of emergence. In this way, Koro-Ljungberg and Ulmer contribute new ways of (re-)thinking 'collaborative writing' within post-qualitative research.

Chapter 8 ("Written Raw: Omissions, Overshares, and the Shameful Ethics of Personal Narrative") opens section 3, with Sophie Tamas re-narrating the pain, politics, and production of the autoethnographic project. Presenting lyrical 'fragments' of memories (re-)made meaningful in the writing of a book project on spousal abuse, Tamas confronts moral and ethical questions concerning secrets, lies, shame, privacy, power, gender, and so forth. In the process, she unsettles "dominant linear Western ways of thinking" and navigates the "absent and unseen" of our lives as it is strewn across the pages in front of us. In complicating the narrative, she draws from the work of Melissa Orlie, Lauren Berlant, and Gilles Deleuze, presenting a messy text through which to make sense of and rethink the boundaries of our writing.

Patricia Leavy follows with chapter 9 ("Writing In/Through the In Between: Messy Middles and Cartoon Clouds"), in which she re-visits (the construction of) her novel, *Low-Fat Love*, and the conditions of emergence that gave rise to the project—as well as how she exists inside/outside/alongside/within/without/over/against the narrative. Weaving the past and personal through sharp prose and drawing on her own experiences (as well as those of her daughter), Leavy carves out space to re-read writing practices and the stories they/we inhabit. In so doing, she engages with and subverts questions of gender, dis/ability, childhood, and the politics of the academy, reveling in the middle-space—the liminal window—the "gap between true and more true."

The volume comes to a close with chapter 10 ("Fragments of a Western Self"), as Norman K. Denzin presents us with a one-act play to create a critical autoethnographic account of the author's histories with his family, the postmodern West, and Native Americans. Invoking the work of Bud Goodall and Greg Ulmer, the films of Guy Maddin, *The Lone Ranger* television show, and Native American history, Denzin (re-)inserts himself into family histories and the sting of childhood memories, seeing and re-discovering the past "not as a succession of events, but as a series of scenes, inventions, emotions, images, and stories." What results is a powerful performance text that contests taken-for-granted assumptions about race, nation, and politics at particular points in U.S. history.

By Way of a Conclusion

Qualitative Inquiry Through a Critical Lens marks the eleventh volume in our series of books that have evolved from the International Congress of Qualitative Inquiry. Last year, we addressed the politics of research and how we might best begin to navigate the messy terrain of academic life in the new normal of a higher education dominated by grant funding, bibliometrics, institutional review boards, and ongoing debates over evidence-based research. The situation has only gotten worse in the intervening year, and there is no reason to think it will get better anytime soon, especially given the tenor of this year's presidential election primary season, which on the Republican side has become license for open assaults on women, racial/ethnic/sexual minorities, higher education, science, and the poor.

Thus, and as we argued in *Qualitative Inquiry—Past, Present, and Future* (Denzin & Giardina, 2015b, pp. 18–20), it is time to open up new spaces, time to explore new discourses. And we need to find new ways of connecting people and their personal troubles with social justice methodologies. We need to become better accomplished in linking these interventions to those institutional sites where troubles are turned into public issues, and public issues transformed into social policy (Charmaz, 2005; Mills, 1959). A critical framework that privileges practice, politics, action, consequences, performances, discourses, methodologies of the heart, pedagogies of hope, love, care, forgiveness, and healing is needed now more so than ever before (see, e.g., Freire, 2001; hooks, 2005; Mills, 1959; Pelias, 2004; West, 1989, 1991). It speaks for and with those who are on the margins. As a liberationist philosophy, it is committed to examining the consequences of racism, poverty, and sexism on the lives of interacting individuals (Seigfried, 1996).

To wit: Each generation must draw its line in the sand and take a stance toward the past.

Each generation must articulate its epistemological, ontological, methodological, and ethical stance toward critical inquiry.

Each generation must offer its responses to current and past criticisms.

We hope our volume contributes to this conversation.

Notes

1 The Allen case is not an outlier. Similar political controversies have occurred in Texas—where the State Board of Education adopted new textbooks that have been widely challenged by historians for, among other things, presenting African slaves as "workers," implying that segregated schools weren't problematic, and declaring "Affirmative Action recipients are un-American" (Haq, 2014, para. 3)—to Virginia, where the approved fourth-grade history textbook claims that "thousands" of Black soldiers fought for the Confederacy (Kehe, 2010).

2 For example, Florida State University recently received a $100 million gift to create the Jim Moran School of Entrepreneurship, a new entity within the university that will be the largest interdisciplinary degree-granting school of entrepreneurship in the United States.

3 Portions of this section are drawn from and revisit Denzin (2010), Denzin and Giardina (2015a), and Giardina (in press).

4 The term 'onto-epistemology' is most often ascribed to Karen Barad (2007), who defines it as "the study of the intertwined practices of knowing and being," thus conjoining 'ontology' and 'epistemology' to mark their "inseparability" (p. 409).

5 Lather and St. Pierre (2013) describe this form of inquiry as such: "This inquiry cannot be tidily described in textbooks or handbooks. There is no methodological instrumentality to be unproblematically learned. In this methodology-to-come, we begin to do it differently wherever we are in our projects" (p. 635).

6 Of course, we are not suggesting that methods are *unimportant*. Rather, and following St. Pierre (2015), it is that we need to get beyond the notion that being technically proficient in methods alone will suffice for conducting critical qualitative inquiry—there needs to be a prolonged, serious engagement with questions of epistemology and ontology.

References

Agamben, G. (1998). *Homo sacer: Sovereign power and bare life*. (Trans. by D. Heller-Roazen). Palo Alto, CA: Stanford University Press.

Ahmed, S. (2006). *Queer phenomenology: Orientations, objects, others*. Durham, NC: Duke University Press.

Alexander, B. K. (2012). *The performative sustainability of race: Reflections on Black culture and the politics of identity*. New York: Peter Lang.

Barad, K. (2007). *Meeting the university halfway: Quantum physics and the entanglement of matter and meaning*. Durham, NC: Duke University Press.

Braidotti, R. (2013). *The posthuman*. New York: Polity.

Brown, W. (2015). *Undoing the demos: Neoliberalism's stealth revolution*. Boston: MIT Press.

Carpenter, Z. (2015, November 16). The University of North Carolina's new president should scare anyone who cares about higher ed. *The Nation*. Retrieved from http://www.thenation.com/article/the-university-of-north-carolinas-new-president-should-scare-anyone-who-cares-about-higher-ed/.

Charis-Carlson, J. (2015, September 25). 5 regents met Bruce Harreld weeks before interview. *Iowa City Press-Citizen*. Retrieved from http://www.press-citizen.com/story/news/education/university-of-iowa/2015/09/24/5-regents-met-harreld-month-before-interviews/72761236/.

Charmaz, K. (2005). Scrutinizing standards: Convergent questions in medical practice and qualitative inquiry. *Symbolic Interaction, 28*(2), 281–289.

Clough, P., with Halley, J. (Eds.) (2007). *The affective turn: Theorizing the social*. Durham, NC: Duke University Press.

Cohen-Cruz, J. (2010). *Engaging performance: Theatre as a call and response*. New York: Routledge.

Conquergood, D. (1991). Rethinking ethnography: Towards a critical cultural politics. *Communication Monographs, 58*(2), 179–194.

Coole, D., & Frost, S. (Eds.) (2010). *New materialisms: Ontology, agency, and politics*. Durham, NC: Duke University Press.

Delaney, E. (2013, December 1). Humanities studies under strain around the globe. *The New York Times*. Retrieved from http://www.nytimes.com/2013/12/02/us/humanities-studies-under-strain-around-the-globe.html.

Denzin, N. K. (2009). *Qualitative inquiry under fire: Toward a new paradigm dialogue.* Walnut Creek, CA: Left Coast Press.

Denzin, N. K. (2010). *The qualitative manifesto: A call to arms.* Walnut Creek, CA: Left Coast Press.

Denzin, N. K., & Giardina, M. D. (Eds.) (2006). *Qualitative inquiry and the conservative challenge.* Walnut Creek, CA: Left Coast Press.

Denzin, N. K., & Giardina, M. D. (Eds.) (2008). *Qualitative inquiry and the politics of evidence.* Walnut Creek, CA: Left Coast Press.

Denzin, N. K., & Giardina, M. D. (Eds.) (2012). *Qualitative inquiry and the politics of advocacy.* Walnut Creek, CA: Left Coast Press.

Denzin, N. K., & Giardina, M. D. (Eds.) (2015a). *Qualitative inquiry and the politics of research.* Walnut Creek, CA: Left Coast Press.

Denzin, N. K., & Giardina, M. D. (Eds.) (2015b). *Qualitative inquiry—past, present, future: A critical reader.* Walnut Creek, CA: Left Coast Press.

Driskill, Q., Finley, C., Gilley, B. J., & Morgensen, S. L. (Eds.) (2011). *Queer indigenous studies: Critical interventions in theory, politics, and literature.* Tucson: University of Arizona Press.

Fenske, M., & Goltz, D. B. (2014). Disciplinary dedications and extradisciplinary experiences: Themes on a relation. *Text and Performance Quarterly, 34,* 1–8.

Fernandez, M., & Montgomery, D. (2015, June 2). Texas lawmakers pass a bill allowing guns at colleges. *The New York Times.* Retrieved from http://www.nytimes.com/2015/06/03/us/texas-lawmakers-approve-bill-allowing-guns-on-campus.html.

Freire, P. (2001). *Pedagogy of the oppressed.* New York: Continuum.

Garoian, C. R., & Gaudelius, Y. M. (2008). *Spectacle pedagogy: Art, politics, and visual culture.* Albany: SUNY Press.

Geertz, C. (1988). *Works and lives: The anthropologist as author.* Palo Alto, CA: Stanford University Press.

Gencarella, S. O., & Pezzullo, P. C. (Eds.) (2010). *Readings on rhetoric and performance.* New York: Strata Press.

Giardina, M. D. (in press). Challenges and opportunities for qualitative research: Future directions. In B. Smith and A. Sparkes (Eds.), *Routledge international handbook of qualitative research in sport and exercise.* London: Routledge.

Giardina, M. D., & Laurendeau, J. (2013). Truth untold? Evidence, knowledge, and research practice(s). *Sociology of Sport Journal, 30,* 237–255.

Giardina, M. D., & Newman, J. I. (2014). The politics of research. In P. Leavy (Ed.), *The Oxford handbook of qualitative research* (pp. 699–723). New York: Oxford University Press.

Giroux, H. A. (2014). *Neoliberalism's war on higher education.* New York: Haymarket.

Gregg, M., & Seigworth, G. J. (Eds.) (2010). *The affect theory reader.* Durham, NC: Duke University Press.

Grove, J. (2015, September 14). Social sciences and humanities faculties 'to close' in Japan after ministerial intervention. *Times Higher Education.* Retrieved from https://www.timeshighereducation.com/news/social-sciences-and-humanities-faculties-close-japan-after-ministerial-intervention.

Haq, H. (2014, September 18). Liberals and conservatives both object to new Texas textbooks. *Christian Science Monitor.* Retrieved from http://www.csmonitor.com/Books/chapter-and-verse/2014/0918/Liberals-and-conservatives-both-object-to-new-Texas-textbooks.

hooks, b. (2005). *Soul sister: Women, friendship, and fulfillment.* Boston: South End Press.

Jackson, A. Y., & Mazzei, L. A. (2012). *Thinking with theory in qualitative research: Viewing data across multiple perspectives.* New York: Routledge.

Johnson, E. P. (2003). *Appropriating blackness: Performance and the politics of authenticity*. Durham, NC: Duke University Press.

Jones, S. H., Adams, T. E., & Ellis, C. (Eds.) (2015). *The handbook of autoethnography*. Walnut Creek, CA: Left Coast Press.

Kehe, M. (2010, October 21). Textbook controversy over claim that Blacks fought for the Confederacy. *The Christian Science Monitor*. Retrieved from http://www.csmonitor.com/Books/chapter-and-verse/2010/1021/Textbook-controversy-over-claim-that-blacks-fought-for-the-Confederacy.

Koro-Ljungberg, M. (2015). *Reconceptualizing qualitative research*. Thousand Oaks, CA: Sage.

Kuppers, P., & Robertson, G. (Eds.) (2007). *The community performance reader*. New York: Routledge.

Lather, P. (2007). *Getting lost: Feminist efforts toward a double(d) science*. Albany: SUNY Press.

Lather, P., & St. Pierre, E. A. (2013). Post-qualitative research. *International Journal of Qualitative Studies in Education, 26*(6), 629–633.

Lincoln, Y. S. (2010). "What a long, strange trip it's been . . ." 25 years of qualitative and new paradigm research. *Qualitative Inquiry, 16*(1), 3–9.

MacLure, M. (2013). Researching without representation? Language and materiality in post-qualitative methodology. *International Journal of Qualitative Studies in Education, 26*(6), 658–667.

Madison, D. S. (2010). *Acts of activism: Human rights as radical performance*. New York: Cambridge University Press.

Mazzei, L. A. (2013). A voice without organs: Interviewing in posthumanist research. *International Journal of Qualitative Studies in Education, 26*, 732–740.

Mills, C. W. (1959). *The sociological imagination*. New York, NY: Oxford University Press.

Norris, J., Sawyer, R. D., & Lund, D. E. (Eds.) (2012). *Duoethnography: Dialogic methods for social, health, and educational research*. Walnut Creek, CA: Left Coast Press.

Pelias, R. J. (2004). *A methodology of the heart*. Walnut Creek, CA: AltaMira Press.

Preston, A. (2015, March 29). The war against humanities at Britain's universities. *The Guardian* (London). Retrieved from http://www.theguardian.com/education/2015/mar/29/war-against-humanities-at-britains-universities.

Purdy, J. (2015, March 19). Ayn Rand comes to U.N.C. *The New Yorker*. Retrieved from http://www.newyorker.com/news/news-desk/new-politics-at-the-university-of-north-carolina.

Rau, A. B. (2015, December 23). Creationist Sylvia Allen to lead Arizona Senate education panel. *The Arizona Republic*. Retrieved from http://www.azcentral.com/story/news/arizona/politics/2015/12/21/arizona-senate-education-panel-sylvia-allen/77720740/.

Saldaña, J. (2011). *Ethnotheatre: Research from page to stage*. Walnut Creek, CA: Left Coast Press.

Schechner, R. (2013). *Performance studies: An introduction* (3/e). New York: Routledge.

Seigfried, C. H. (1996). *Pragmatism and feminism*. Chicago: University of Chicago Press.

Spry, T. (2011). *Body, paper, stage: Writing and performing autoethnography*. Walnut Creek, CA: Left Coast Press.

St. Pierre, E. A. (2011). Post qualitative research: The critique and the coming after. In N. K. Denzin and Y. S. Lincoln (Eds.), *The SAGE handbook of qualitative research* (pp. 611–626), 4/e. Thousand Oaks, CA: Sage.

St. Pierre, E. A. (2013). The posts continue: Becoming. *International Journal of Qualitative Studies in Education, 26*(6), 646–657.

St. Pierre, E. A. (2015). Practices for the 'new' in the new empiricisms, the new material-isms, and post qualitative inquiry. In N. K. Denzin and M. D. Giardina (Eds.), *Qualitative inquiry and the politics of research* (pp. 75–96). Walnut Creek, CA: Left Coast Press.

Strauss, V. (2015, November 14). Naming of Margaret Spellings as new UNC system president called a 'disturbing new low.' *Washington Post*. https://www.washingtonpost.com/news/answer-sheet/wp/2015/11/14/naming-of-margaret-spellings-as-unc-system-president-called-a-disturbing-new-low/.

Warner, M. (2015, March 19). Learning my less. *London Review of Books*. Retrieved from http://www.lrb.co.uk/v37/n06/marina-warner/learning-my-lesson.

Wasserman, E. (2015, December 30). Harreld selection: A tale of two searches. *Iowa City Press-Citizen*. Retrieved from http://www.press-citizen.com/story/opinion/contributors/guest-editorials/2015/09/30/harreld-selection-tale-two-searches/73024712/.

West, C. (1989). *The American evasion of philosophy: A genealogy of pragmatism*. Madison: University of Wisconsin Press.

West, C. (1991). Theory, pragmatism, and politics. In J. Arac and B. Johnson (Eds.), *Consequences of theory* (pp. 22–38). Baltimore, MD: Johns Hopkins University Press.

Woodhouse, K. (2015, December 16). Unprepared professors 'should be shot'? *Inside Higher Ed*. Retrieved from https://www.insidehighered.com/news/2015/12/16/university-iowa-leader-apologizes-saying-teachers-without-lesson-plans-should-be.

Wyatt, J., Gale, J., Gannon, S., & Davies, B. (2011). *Deleuze & collaborative writing: An immanent plane of composition*. New York: Peter Lang.

SECTION I
Theoretical Imperatives

1

THE LONG REACH OF LOGICAL POSITIVISM / LOGICAL EMPIRICISM

Elizabeth Adams St. Pierre

Positivism, indeed, has a long reach: from the positive philosophy—a positivist sociology—of Auguste Comte in the nineteenth century; to the logical positivism / logical empiricism of the Vienna Circle in the early twentieth century; to the scientifically based and evidence-based research (SBR, EBR) in the social sciences, especially in education, at the beginning of the twenty-first century. Throughout its history, positivism has been critiqued and fallen out of favor only to gain traction again when foundations are threatened and things seem too "loose," too contingent.

My first serious encounter with logical positivism or logical empiricism (I'll use these terms interchangeably though there are differences in their meaning) was in 2002 when the editor of the American Educational Research Association (AERA) journal, *Educational Researcher*, invited me to respond to a manuscript (Feuer, Towne, & Shavelson, 2002) she'd received that was an interpretation of the National Research Council's 2002 report *Scientific Research in Education*. I agreed to write a paper (St. Pierre, 2002) in response, though, at the time, I had only a vague understanding of logical positivism and knew almost nothing about the National Academy of Sciences and its operating arm, the National Research Council (NRC), which organizes hundreds of committees of experts to investigate all sorts of issues in the natural and social sciences at the request of Congress and others and which publishes many, many reports, some of which fade away pretty quickly, making little impact. But this particular report, *Scientific Research in Education*, made a huge impact on educational research and practice. I read the manuscript submitted to *Educational Researcher,* read the NRC report, and was appalled. I knew enough about logical positivism to know that the committee of experts who wrote the report had recommended that educational research become even more positivist than it already was in order to be *scientific*.

The U.S. No Child Left Behind Act (NCLB), which was signed into law in 2002, also included a positivist definition of "scientifically based research" in education. What's interesting is that the person who wrote that definition of scientifically based research (i.e., Robert Sweet, professional staff member of the House Education and Workforce Committee), which first appeared in the Reading Excellence Act of 1999 and was elaborated in NCLB, was neither an educator nor a researcher. When interviewed (see Eisenhart & Towne, 2003), Sweet reported he had talked with educational psychologists, who are generally trained in positivist methods, about what should count as "scientific" educational research. If he had talked with interpretive, critical, and postmodern researchers, it is likely he would have written a different definition. Nonetheless, his narrow definition had the force of federal law in NCLB and was then reinforced by Grover Whitehurst, the first director of the Institute of Education Sciences created by NCLB, the new federal agency that would henceforth fund educational research.

The science described in NCLB and the NRC report is grounded in the positivist assumption that the methods of the natural sciences can and should be used in the human sciences. This positivist claim, the unified theory of science, is illustrated in the NRC (2002) report with this statement: "At its core, scientific inquiry is the same in all fields" (p. 2). Once educational inquiry becomes a positivist science using positivist methods, the knowledge that counts is knowledge—preferably mathematical—produced through counting and measuring various issues related to children, teachers, parents, administrators, classrooms, and so on. Whitehurst insisted that only causal research can tell us "what works" in schools and that the best kind of causal research is the randomized controlled trial. Thus, the Institute of Education Sciences decided to fund only causal research, thereby controlling educational research through his funding agency. Because qualitative methodology has typically been interpretive and not causal, it did not qualify for funding.

What is particularly irksome and, I would argue, unethical and unscientific is that, after 15 years of critique of SBR from many educational researchers and practitioners, the recent reauthorization of NCLB—the Every Student Succeeds Act (ESSA), signed into law by President Barack Obama in December 2015—continues to privilege causal research. Note its tiers of evidence below:

- Strong evidence: includes at least one well-designed and well-implemented experimental study, meaning a randomized controlled trial.
- Moderate evidence: includes at least one well-designed and well-implemented quasi-experimental study, like a regression discontinuity analysis.
- Promising evidence: includes at least one well-designed and well-implemented correlational study that controls for selection bias.

In a masterly stroke of revisionist history, Whitehurst (as cited in Sparks, 2015), who seemed to delight in enforcing positivist research during his six-year tenure as director of the Institute of Education Sciences, recently commented, "One error of NCLB was demanding the use of [scientifically based research] when it didn't exist, thus debasing the currency. Another was getting Congress into the business of defining SBR in education—research methodologists they are not. . . . Perhaps these were justified at the time because the state of education research was really awful. But neither makes sense today." The awful research he referred to, as he told educational researchers at the time, was qualitative research and any inquiry that smacked of postmodernism (see St. Pierre, 2006). The installation of positivism in education in 2002 through federal law and a federal funding agency is only one example of the long reach of logical positivism / logical empiricism.

What spurred me to take a more careful look at logical positivism / logical empiricism was an encounter a year later, in 2003, at the AERA conference in Chicago, when I talked with a member of the National Research Council committee who wrote that report on scientifically based research in education. I asked him whether he thought qualitative research was scientific, and he responded, "Qualitative research operates in the context of discovery, not the context of justification, so it's pre-scientific; it's not science." I was shocked at his easy dismissal of qualitative methodology.

But because I really didn't understand what he'd said about the contexts of discovery and justification and so didn't know how to respond, I decided it was imperative that I study logical positivism / logical empiricism, and so began several years of reading I wish I had begun when I was a doctoral student. During those years of studying logical positivism, I wrote journal articles, organized conference sessions, and wrote conference papers defending qualitative methodology from the positivist police. By 2005, which was the first year of the International Congress of Qualitative Inquiry, we qualitative researchers who were under attack were very happy to have a conference of our own, a site for organization and resistance. I remember asking Norman Denzin that first year how many people had registered for the conference and was surprised that about 550 people had come from all over the world. Clearly, we qualitative methodologists needed to talk with each other, and there were many conference sessions in Illinois during the first decade of the twenty-first century in which we tried to figure out what had happened to interpretive qualitative methodology, how it happened, who had the power to make it happen, and how we could resist the twenty-first century attack by neo-positivism.

Eventually, however, I got pretty cranky about having to defend qualitative methodology, for three reasons. First, I believed it was a legitimate, valid form of inquiry if one used humanist interpretive and critical theories that did not need to be defended. But second, much qualitative research was positivized during those years as researchers tried to get funding and make their qualitative studies more "scientific." I could not defend positivist qualitative inquiry. Third, I was weary of defending a form of inquiry that *had never actually worked for me*, attached as I was to postmodern and poststructural theories that critiqued not only the very idea of method and methodology but also the ontology and epistemology of that methodology. How could I believe in what I've called conventional humanist qualitative methodology after reading Derrida, who deconstructed the idea of *presence* on which qualitative methodology depends (being face-to-face in the natural setting), or Foucault, whose analyses were not grounded in the speaking subject (e.g., interviews), or Lyotard, who rejected any idea of method, or Deleuze, whose image of thought could not accommodate the humanist methodologies we've invented.

What struck me during those years of resisting logical positivism / logical empiricism was that many qualitative methodologists, like me, didn't recognize positivism when they saw it. Why? I think those of us who have our doctorates are pretty good, dutiful students, and we learn what we're taught. But I doubt we teach logical positivism / logical empiricism in research methodology curriculum, so why would we know its language, its concepts, and its assumptions about epistemology and ontology? Its methodology has become so normalized that we just take it for granted as real and true. My chief concern about research methodology has been and is that in the rush to application, in the leap to methodology, our university research curricula seldom focus on what we need to understand *before* we study methodology.

I have a telling example of the rush to application. Several years ago, I was invited to serve as a mentor for the Qualitative Research SIG at the AERA conference. What this involved was sitting at a table for a couple of hours with mostly doctoral students coming to talk with me every 15 minutes or so. When I asked them about their research, every single one responded with something like, "I'm doing a grounded study," or "I'm doing a case study," or "I'm doing a cross case analysis." They leaped not just to methodology but to research design. I was completely taken aback. When I asked about the theories that guided their studies, *they* were taken aback and stumbled for an answer. It really came home to me then what we were and were not teaching in our educational research curriculum.

What I mean here is that we seldom teach the history of empiricism or the history of ontology or the philosophy and history of science and social science so that we have that larger understanding of the various grids of intelligibility in which different methodologies are thinkable. I believe I should have been able, and that my students should be able, to reply to that committee member's comment about the contexts of discovery and justification because that idea is a major tenet of logical empiricism—which is everywhere, everywhere. If we agree with Steinmetz (2005) that logical empiricism is the epistemological unconscious of the U.S. social sciences—that logical empiricism is the norm, the given, the unstated, and true—then we should study it very carefully so we can recognize it and its language and assumptions, analyze how it is produced and maintained, track how it functions, and study its effects. In other words, we should understand the enabling conditions in which it is possible to say, as that committee member said to me, that qualitative methodology is pre-scientific because it exists in the context of discovery. But we have *to teach* logical positivism / logical empiricism in our research curriculum to denaturalize it and situate it among other available empiricisms. It should not be "normal," the given.

So what are some of the assumptions of logical positivism / logical empiricism? Here I briefly describe a few assumptions I learned during those years of reading, which I now teach in my theory and methodology courses so my students can recognize it and understand where this belief, this ideology, came from; who invented it and why; how it gained such a hold in the U.S. social sciences; and why it's so attractive to so many.

First of all, it's important to remember that empiricism is an *epistemological project* about the nature, source, and limits of knowledge. Traditionally, debates in epistemology occur between rationalists and empiricists about how dependent knowledge is on sense experience. Those who believe our minds can produce true knowledge apart from the material world are rationalists (in the tradition of the Continental rationalists—i.e., Descartes, Spinoza, and Leibniz), and those who believe true knowledge must be grounded in sensory experiences are empiricists (in the tradition of the British empiricists—i.e., Locke, Berkeley, and Hume). Rationalists are interested in the speculative and metaphysical, the philosophical (ideas), while empiricists dismiss knowledge unless it is grounded in scientific facts, scientific evidence gathered in the "real" world from observation, for example. In this way, empiricism becomes a theoretical framework for knowledge production in the human sciences. However, it is important to recognize that empiricism itself is only an idea, a theory, and not the truth and that it is thinkable only in a mind/body dualism.

A brief story about logical positivism / logical empiricism goes something like this (see also St. Pierre, 2012). Near the beginning of the twentieth century, a group of European mathematicians, philosophers, sociologists, economists, and scientists met in Vienna to discuss philosophy of science and epistemology and began several projects (e.g., the *International Encyclopedia of Unified Sciences*, the last volume of which was Thomas Kuhn's [first edition, 1962] *Structure of Scientific Revolutions*). They fled Vienna and Europe when the Nazis came to power before World War II. In universities in Britain and the United States, where they were welcomed, they continued to develop logical positivism / logical empiricism. They believed that speculative philosophy not grounded in scientific facts had led to the two world wars, and their work to decontaminate science from contingency, from doubt, and from any kind of metaphysics intensified. Social science disciplines like sociology, economics, psychology, and political science embraced logical positivism and its reliance on mathematical (objective) knowledge rather than value-laden (biased) knowledge to make what were arguably the soft social sciences harder, more like physics, the hardest of the hard sciences.

A chief tenet of logical positivism / logical empiricism is that the knowledge that counts is what can be counted, measured, quantified, and reduced to numbers. We see this play out in schools where we try to measure everything—knowledge, intelligence, aptitude, behavior, and so on. We have, in fact, quantified students and teachers, but this was exactly the intention of scientifically based research in education. Positivists assume that our measurements and quantifications have predictive capabilities so that we can, with confidence, predict how a child will perform in the real world in the future. The logic here is that if we can predict what will happen, we can control it through interventions that will *cause* a change. Logical positivism / logical empiricism relies on the logic of causation. And all of this is deemed theory-free, value-free, scientific. What children and teachers say and believe can't be measured and so exists in the context of discovery (pre-scientific). Only that which can be objectively, scientifically analyzed exists in the context of justification (scientific). The assumptions that enable that distinction are *beliefs*, so, from the beginning, logical positivism is only an idea, not the truth as it claims.

Another tenet of logical positivism / logical empiricism is a belief in incrementalism, the idea that knowledge steadily accumulates so that we are always making progress toward more adequate knowledge. We see incrementalism in social science research when researchers are asked to identify a gap in knowledge to study. The assumption is that bits of knowledge are like bricks that form a foundation that secures true knowledge about something—the truth about dropouts, the truth about happiness, the truth about good marriages. Kuhn (1970) wrote that scientists like to think that knowledge production is a linear process and that they are progressing toward certainty but that there is little evidence that this is so. He argued that scientists are generally ahistorical and that incrementalism is mostly an effect of textbooks that smooth out so-called gaps to present certain kinds of knowledge as secure. Incrementalism does not explain how what is considered a scientific fact today can, in 10 or 20 years, be rejected as a mistake. And, as Hacking (1983) wrote, "there can be heapings up of knowledge without there being any unity of science to which they all add up. There can also be an increasing depth of understanding and breadth of generalization without anything properly called convergence" (pp. 55–56).

Logical positivism / logical empiricism is, of course, grounded in the Cartesian *cogito*, a description of being, and of human being, that employs the self/other, mind/body, objective/subjective, reason/emotion, human/nonhuman, human/ material binaries. With Descartes, *to be* becomes *to know*. In a sleight of hand— *cogito ergo sum*—our projects become epistemological and knowledge our aim. Humans become separate from and superior to the world. Only humans have language and can speak and think and produce knowledge, and the world is passive, inert matter waiting to be known. Our responsibility is to master the world, to analyze it scientifically in order to separate what is contingent and speculative from what is value-free and true. This belief plays out in social science research when researchers are told to be objective and free of bias. In qualitative research, they are often asked to write "subjectivity statements" that identify their attachments, values, and experiences that are likely to contaminate their projects, as if one can step outside oneself to analyze oneself.

Logical positivism / logical empiricism also argues that language can and must be brute, perfectly clear, and so scientific (see Ayer, 1936). Words mean what they say. The logic of representation undergirds this assumption, the idea that language is transparent and can accurately represent or reproduce something, that language is really not there. As Baudrillard (1988) wrote, "All of Western faith and good faith was engaged in this wager on representation: that a sign could refer to the depth of meaning, that a sign could exchange for meaning and that something could guarantee the exchange" (p. 5), something transcendental. Logical positivists often call postmodern work "deliberately obfuscatory" because it focuses more on how language works than on what it "means," and they dismiss postmodern writing as *jargon*, ignoring the fact that logical positivism / logical empiricism has its own special language that could be called jargon. Positivism influences qualitative researchers when they focus on capturing the exact words spoken by participants and on reproducing in their reports large portions of interviews word for word (e.g., data dumps), claiming that the "data speak for themselves," as if the words are brute, perfectly clear. Here, the researcher refuses to interpret, to analyze, and assumes that participants' words are not always already interpretations most often produced within the dominant discourse.

Twenty-first-century logical positivism / logical empiricism appears to be scientism's latest fad. Scientism itself has a long history, going back to the sixteenth century, a history in which science is always deemed superior, not only to philosophy but to all of culture. Scientism is the worship of science, especially the natural sciences; it is the belief that science is the final arbiter of everything—when in doubt, do science on it, measure it, mathematize it, scientize it. Sorell (1991) explained that scientism also includes the idea that "it is always good for subjects that do not belong to science [e.g., education] to be placed on a scientific footing" (p. 1). Habermas (1971) believed that positivism cannot be thought without scientism. Not only did logical positivism separate science from philosophy and consider it superior, it helped create the "human sciences," scientizing not only nature but also humanity. Hence, we have social science, education science, political science, and so on. Foucault (1970) helped us understand this new "order of things," the invention of the human sciences.

Much early educational research was accomplished by those trained in the logical positivism / logical empiricism of the behavioral sciences, especially educational psychology. That logical empiricism had, and still has, a great influence on what counts as rigorous, high-quality scientific research, especially in education. If you've studied logical empiricism / logical positivism and then read that research carefully, it's easy to identify it as logical positivist / logical empiricist.

But qualitative methodology was invented in the 1970s and 1980s as an *interpretive* social science methodology to critique the excesses of logical positivism—its measurement mentality, its trust in numbers, and its belief that scientific method can be the final arbiter of meaning. Unfortunately, what is presumed to be interpretive or critical qualitative methodology has never been able to free itself from the methods-driven, objective approach of logical positivism / logical empiricism. For example, when qualitative researchers write "subjectivity statements" to identify their *bias*, when they employ *triangulation* to hone in on the truth, and when they believe that *member checks* can correct discrepancies in their interpretations, they rely on logical positivism's presumed objectivity to produce validity. When researchers explain the gap in knowledge their studies will fill, they appeal to positivism's incrementalism, the idea that knowledge accumulates. When they use the concept *data collection*, they assume that data exist independent of people such that they can be "collected," thus adopting the human/nonhuman distinction of logical positivism / logical empiricism. When they *code data*, they assume that words can contain and close off meaning, that words can be *brute data*, adopting logical positivism's view of language. When they forego narrative and description in their social science research reports and present data as one would in a natural science report, they emulate logical positivism / logical empiricism. When they rely on practices of formalization and systematicity to guarantee rigor, they mimic a simulacrum of the natural sciences.

Logical positivism / logical empiricism has had great staying power, but since the neo-positivist restoration at the beginning of the twentieth century, the soft social sciences have tried even harder to be hard like the natural sciences even though, as Nelson (1997) wrote, "the story [logical positivism / logical empiricism] told about scientific investigation failed, almost completely, to match the actual practices of scientists" (p. 60). We know that the supposed hard, objective, rational, observation-dependent, measurement-driven, replicable natural sciences the soft social scientists continue to try to duplicate was and is, indeed, a simulacrum, a reality that does not exist. The natural sciences are as value-laden as the social sciences, and objectivity is an illusion. No scientists, either natural or social, can simply disappear from their studies; they cannot not be there. As Haraway (1988) reminded us, there is no God's-eye view from nowhere, and all knowledge is situated.

As far as the privileging of observation—central to empirical work in both the natural and the social sciences—is concerned, Clough (2009) wrote that the "naturalistic method of observation presumes the obdurateness of the empirical world, or the independence of the empirical world from interpretation" (p. 46). But in physics, Niels Bohr explained decades ago that, at the quantum level, there could be no distinction between the object and the experimental circumstances that permitted the object to be observed, that the observer and the object make up an interacting unit. And given that science demands that our observations be textualized, we might remember Foucault's (1970) caution: "*It is in vain that we say what we see; what we see never resides in what we say*" (p. 11, emphasis added by author). In other words, language simply can't do the work the logical positivists / logical empiricists want it to do—it can't clearly mirror, capture, and represent an observed reality.

A hallmark of valid social science research, mimicking the natural sciences, is replication. But in a recent front-page article in the *New York Times*, Carey (2015,

p. A1) reported, "The past several years have been bruising ones for the credibility of social sciences." He continued,

> A painstaking yearslong effort to reproduce 100 studies published in three leading psychology journals has found that more than half of the findings did not hold up when retested. The analysis was done by research psychologists, many of whom volunteered their time to double check what they considered important work . . . More than 60 of the studies did not hold up. . . . Dr. John Ionnidis, a director of Stanford University's Meta-Research Innovation Center, who once estimated that about half of published results across medicine were inflated or wrong, noted the proportion in psychology was even larger than he had thought. He said the problem could be even worse in other fields.

Lather (2015, personal communication) noted that replication has always been the Achilles heel of logical positivism / logical empiricism because it is highly unlikely that any research with people—who are not inanimate, static, and stable—can be replicated. Even in the natural sciences, in the hardest of the hard sciences, physics, it is increasingly impossible to reproduce complex, fleeting experimental conditions and events. Why, then, would we expect to replicate the complexity of the social world? Nothing stands still for repetition. We have to ask what, then, *are* the criteria for rigorous social science research, a question that, I would argue, positivism has wrongly answered, and, in doing so, it has damaged real people.

Logical positivism / logical empiricism fails on many fronts, and no one wants to be called a positivist; nonetheless, its long reach in the social science continues. In educational research, we now have positivist qualitative methodology. Whatever was loose, complex, emergent, and interpretive has been formalized, systematized, and tightened up for science's sake. In schools we now have data rooms whose walls are lined with charts with sticky notes representing individual children on graphs. Schools have data meetings during which faculty discuss the explosion of data they collect—numbers that represent what cannot be measured. Using logical positivism / logical empiricism, we've produced measured and quantified students and teachers.

And yet I expect few classroom teachers or administrators and, unfortunately, few educational researchers can identify the empiricism that drives that kind of research, its practices, and its effects. I think logical positivism / logical empiricism remains the epistemological unconsciousness of the social sciences. It has become so taken-for-granted and normalized that rather than having to justify using it given its profound failures, we have to justify using other empiricisms enabled by different images of thought that are profoundly promising.

As I wrote earlier, I believe we need to study logical positivism / logical empiricism *and teach it* so we can recognize it when we see it, so we can bring it out into the open in order to counter all those *beliefs* it privileges, which are not the truth.

I'll list some of its claims again here at the end: the belief in scientism (the idea that true knowledge comes from science and not from metaphysics and philosophy); a belief in the unity of science (that the methods of the natural sciences can be applied to the social sciences); a belief that rigorous science has predictive capabilities; a belief in objectivity (that inquiry can be value-free); a reliance on objective observation and measurement (the idea that the human is separate from the natural world); a trust in numbers; a belief in incrementalism (that knowledge steadily accumulates); the idea that language can be transparent and unambiguous; the idea that rigorous research can be replicated. When we see these claims being made either directly or indirectly, we should recognize that logical positivism / logical empiricism is being employed. All of us should recognize it when we see it, especially our students who will be the next generation of empirical researchers. My desires are, first, that we study the historical and philosophical conditions in which various empiricisms become thinkable, that we understand the assumptions that structure them, and that we study their possibilities and limits. I would call *that* work—not some pre-given, normalized, systematized, methods-driven work—the beginning of rigorous inquiry.

References

Ayer, A.J. (1936). *Language, truth, and logic.* London: Victor Gollancz, Ltd.

Baudrillard, J. (1988). Simulacra and simulations. In M. Poster (Ed.), *Jean Baudrillard: Selected writings* (P. Foss, P. Patton, & P. Beitchman, Trans.) (pp. 166–184). Stanford, CA: Stanford University Press. (Original work published 1981).

Carey, B. (2015, August 28). Many psychology findings not as strong as claimed, study says. *New York Times*, p. A1.

Clough, P. T. (2009). The new empiricism: Affect and sociological method. *European Journal of Social Theory, 12*(1): 43–61.

Deleuze, G., & Guattari, F. (1987). *A thousand plateaus: Capitalism and schizophrenia.* (B. Massumi, Trans.). Minneapolis: University of Minnesota Press. (Original work published 1980).

Eisenhart, M, & Towne, L. (2003). Contestation and change in national policy on "scientifically based" education research. *Educational Researcher, 32*(7), 31–38.

Feuer, M. J., Towne, L., & Shavelson, R. J. (2002). Scientific culture and educational research. *Educational Researcher 31*(8), 4–14.

Foucault, M. (1970). *The order of things: An archaeology of the human sciences.* (A.M.S. Smith, Trans.). New York: Vintage Books. (Original work published 1966).

Habermas, J. (1971). *Knowledge and human interests* (J. J. Shapiro, Trans.). Boston: Beacon Press. (Original work published 1968).

Hacking, Ian. (1983*). Representing and intervening: Introductory topics in the philosophy of natural science.* Cambridge, UK: Cambridge University Press.

Haraway, D. J. (1988). Situated knowledges: The science question in feminism and the privilege of partial perspective. *Feminist Studies, 14*(3), 575–599.

Kuhn, T. S. (1962, 1970). *The structure of scientific revolutions.* (2nd ed.). Chicago: University of Chicago Press.

National Research Council. (2002). *Scientific research in education*. (R.J. Shavelson & L. Towne, Eds.). Committee on Scientific Principles for Education Research. Washington, DC: National Academies Press.

Nelson, J. (1997). The last dogma of empiricism. In L. H. Nelson & J. Nelson (Eds.), *Feminism, science, and the philosophy of science* (pp. 59–78). Dordrecht, Netherlands: Kluwer Academic Publishers.

Sorell, T. (1991). *Scientism: Philosophy and the infatuation with science*. London: Routledge.

Sparks, S. D. (2015, December 4). What role will research play in ESSA? *Education Week*. http://blogs.edweek.org/edweek/inside-school-research/2015/12/essa_waves_at_tiered_evidence.html.

Steinmetz, G. (2005) The epistemological unconscious of U.S. sociology and the transition to post-Fordism: The case of historical sociology. In J. Adams, E. S. Clemens, & A.S. Orloff (Eds.), *Remaking modernity: Politics, history, sociology* (pp. 109–157). Durham, NC: Duke University Press.

St. Pierre, E.A. (2002). "Science" rejects postmodernism. *Educational Researcher, 31*(8), 25–27.

St. Pierre, E.A. (2006). Scientifically based research in education: Epistemology and ethics. *Adult Education Quarterly, 56*(4), 239–266.

St. Pierre, E.A. (2012). Another postmodern report on knowledge: Positivism and its others. *International Journal of Leadership in Education, 15*(4), 483–503.

2

MOVING FORWARD, PUSHING BACK

Indigenous Methodologies in the Academy

Margaret Kovach

Good Afternoon.[1] It is an honour to be here with you today. Before I begin my talk, I would like to offer acknowledgements and greetings. I would like to start by acknowledging the ancestral caretakers of this land. Through a statement collectively crafted by the Indigenous Inquiries Circle of the International Congress of Qualitative Inquiry, I acknowledge the land upon which we gather for the Eleventh International Congress of Qualitative Inquiry:

> These lands were the traditional territory of a number of First Nations bands prior to European contact, with the Peoria, Kaskaskia, Piankashaw, Wea, Miami, Mascoutin, Odawa, Sauk, Mesquakie, Kickapoo, Potawatomi, and Chippewa people being some of the last bands forcibly removed. This land witnessed many First Peoples' resistance against the pressures of colonization manifested through war, disease, and diaspora. These lands carry that memory through the stories of the people and the struggle for survival and identity in the face of overwhelming colonizing power.
>
> *(Acknowledging the Land, 2013, n.p)*

I would like to acknowledge the elders, knowledge-holders, leaders, teachers, learners, colleagues, and friends who are here today. I would like to acknowledge all of the organizers and those who have provided support for this conference. I would also like to give special acknowledgement to the Indigenous Inquiries Circle of this conference. I have had the opportunity to be a part of this group since its inception in 2011. It has been rewarding to see the Indigenous Inquiries Circle grow, and each year I look forward to the spirit, humour, and good feeling of this group as we work to uphold Indigenous research processes.

My name is Margaret Kovach, and I am of Plains Cree and Saulteaux ancestry. I am a member of Pasqua First Nations, a First Nation community located in southern Saskatchewan, Canada. My ancestors were signatories to Treaty Four. I currently live in Saskatoon (in Treaty Six territory) with my family, where I am a faculty member in the College of Education at the University of Saskatchewan.

By way of an introduction, I would like to share with you information about my home province and country that has relevance for Indigenous inquiries and education in my context. Indigenous peoples in my country are not vanishing by any means. Canada's Aboriginal population is growing faster than the general population. Between 1996 and 2006, the Aboriginal population grew by 45%, whereas the non-Aboriginal population grew by 8% (Statistics Canada, 2010). The Canadian Plains Research Centre projects that the Aboriginal population will be 33% of the total Saskatchewan population by 2045 (Anderson, 2007). By 2016, 45% of students entering kindergarten in Saskatchewan will be of Aboriginal ancestry (Saskatchewan School Boards Association, 2009).

The demographics in Canada reflect a growing Indigenous presence. It is with a sense of excitement and possibility that I consider twenty-first-century education and research. It is also with recognition that there is continued need for justice and equity for Indigenous peoples. This means that we must work toward creating an understanding of Indigenous communities, knowledges, and methodologies on their own terms.

The theme of this year's conference is "Constructing a New Critical Qualitative Inquiry." We are being asked to reflect upon what changes have occurred in qualitative inquiry over the past decade and century. The organizers of the conference have asked us to consider the following questions: What might the International Congress of Qualitative Inquiry look like at its twentieth anniversary (i.e., 10 years from now)? What have we learned? Where do we go next (Denzin, 2015)? As I consider this question, immediately I see the field of qualitative inquiry influenced by the protocols of respect, relevance, and responsibility found within the philosophical foundations of Indigenous knowledges and Indigenous methodologies. In my mind the future landscape of qualitative inquiry and research does not simply include Indigenous methodologies but is influenced by the Indigenous spirit of relationally relevant research. As we move forward I see there are at least three challenges facing Indigenous methodologies. The three challenges include the following: the need to raise consciousness about Indigenous methodologies as a distinctive methodological approach to research; the criticality of understanding and enacting the relational underpinnings of Indigenous research; and a sustained effort toward pushing back against domesticating norms of Western intellectual tradition that moves with neo-colonial tendencies. I would like to address these three challenges today.

First, I would like to start by reaffirming the need to continue to raise awareness of Indigenous methodologies. The research community (both inside and outside the academy) must become aware of the principles and practices that guide this distinctive approach. I was as a doctoral student in 2003 when I first started to think specifically about the nature of research methodology grounded within Indigenous knowledge systems. At that time, Linda Tuhiwai Smith's book, *Decolonizing Methodologies* (first edition), had been published four years prior in 1999. In 2003, there were only a few articles, such as "What Is an Indigenous Research Methodology?" written by Cree scholar Dr. Shawn Wilson (2001), which articulated the naming of Indigenous Methodologies. His book *Research Is Ceremony—Indigenous Research Methods* (2008) was not yet published. About 10 to 15 years ago, Indigenous methodologies in academic research discourses were newly emergent and known to a select few. Since that time there has been a consistent, sustained movement of research projects, discourses, and publications integrating these approaches.

In twenty-first-century qualitative inquiry, all of those involved in the teaching and discourses of qualitative inquiry should, at minimum, recognize Indigenous methodologies as a legitimate qualitative approach and be conversant enough to know what it involves. For this to happen, those of us involved in Indigenous methodologies have some educating to do. It is our responsibility to our Indigenous ancestors and the future generations. It is work that we must do. The general qualitative research community has the responsibility to become aware.

In an effort to walk my talk, I would like to offer a very brief overview of Indigenous methodologies beginning with the foundational premise that this approach is distinct and unique within qualitative research. To make this point, I would like to share with you a recent Indigenous methodology success story that has been in several provincial and national Canadian newspapers this spring. The headline of the *Saskatoon Star Phoenix* article of May 8, 2015, reads, "Student Writes 52,438-Word Dissertation With No Punctuation" (Hutchinson, 2015).

In April of 2015, Dr. Patrick Robert Reid Stewart of the Nisga'a nation successfully defended his doctoral defense at the University of British Columbia. Dr. Stewart's (2015) interdisciplinary doctoral thesis is entitled *Indigenous Architecture Through Indigenous Knowledge: Dim sagalts'apkw nisim [Together we will build a Village]*. His doctoral research integrated an Indigenous methodological approach. Very briefly, Dr. Stewart first submitted his thesis in Nisga'a, but it was not accepted. He was asked to translate his dissertation into the English language. He subsequently translated the dissertation from Nisga'a to English text but remained committed to the spirit of orality. The dissertation as written is an honouring of the spoken word. In the preface of the dissertation, he explains his style:

> [T]he formatting and punctuation or lack thereof, has grown out of my need to privilege Indigenous knowledge in resistance to the colonizing provincial education system that continue to traumatize indigenous peoples in this province. The following adaawak [story or teaching] about teaching adult indigenous learners contextualizes the need for a discursive space to

privilege an indigenous methodology. You, the reader, will notice a change in writing style from standard or conventional academic English to one you may be quite unfamiliar with, but read it as if i am speaking directly to your heart.

(pp. xi)

No doubt, Stewart's work suggests both the possibilities and the concessions for those of us engaged in Indigenous methodologies. However, it cannot be denied that Indigenous methodologies create "discursive space" to heed the drumbeat of our peoples. In his dissertation he cites the assertion put forward by Denzin, Lincoln, and Smith that through privileging Indigenous knowledges such research is grounded in "an oppositional consciousness that resists 'neocolonizing postmodern global formations'" (as cited in Stewart, 2015, pp. viii). I acknowledge Stewart's doctoral work and the support of his committee because it represents a recent example of Indigenous methodologies that pushes back against a Western intellectual imperialism through keeping the memory of our knowledges alive.

In the past several years I have had experience in a number of capacities to think about Indigenous research—as a researcher and as a participant of research integrating Indigenous methodologies; as a graduate supervisor of students taking up Indigenous methodologies; as an instructor of an Indigenous research course for a period of seven years; as an Indigenous research grant adjudicator; as a community Aboriginal research advisory board member; this past year as the Acting Academic Director of the Aboriginal Education Research Centre; and as a member of the Indigenous Inquiries Circle of this conference. I share this with you to indicate that I have had the opportunity to consider Indigenous research and methodologies from a number of perspectives over a period of time. Through these experiences I have had the great privilege of being in conversation with many individuals who care deeply about Indigenous peoples and communities. These individuals wish to see research with Indigenous peoples conducted in an ethical manner that benefits Indigenous community. From these experiences, this is what I have learned about Indigenous methodologies.

Foremost, when we consider Indigenous methodologies we must begin with the understanding that this research approach is guided by Indigenous knowledge systems. This point is critical in understanding Indigenous methodologies. Words evoked when we consider Indigenous methodologies include animistic, relational, collective, contextual and place-based, spiritual, holistic, experiential. However, all of these words and understandings must be grounded within an understanding of Indigenous worldview and community. I particularly like this quote by Bird-David in referencing an Indigenous worldview:

Knowing . . . grows from and is [about] maintaining relatedness with neighboring others. It involves dividuating the environment rather than dichotomoizing it and turning attention to "we-ness," which absorbs differences, rather than to "otherness," which highlights differences and eclipses commonalities. Against "I think, therefore I am" stand "I relate, therefore I am" and "I know as I relate."

(1999, p. 78)

If only one understanding is to be garnered about Indigenous methodologies, it must be this: It is not possible to engage in Indigenous methodologies without a knowledge base in Indigenous knowledge systems and community relations. To do so is to undertake a methodology, but it is not Indigenous.

The following are some specifics that may help to clarify features of an Indigenous methodological approach. This is not necessarily a "checklist," but the long and short of it is that if a researcher wishes to engage an Indigenous methodology, the collective wisdom by those involved in the Indigenous research community suggests that the following aspects must be in place.

First off, Indigenous research is not *ad hoc* or arbitrary. It is grounded in Indigeniety. There must be Indigenous people on the research team in some capacity (researchers, elders, community advisory board members, community researchers, or a combination thereof). Throughout the process there is respect and acknowledgement of those who have influenced our thinking and supported our being. There must be more than surface, rhetorical understanding of Indigenous knowledges. The researchers will need to show that they have a sophisticated understanding of Indigenous knowledge systems and can speak to aspects of an Indigenous worldview.

There is evidence of respectful contextual knowledge about the Indigenous peoples that the research involves. This includes a sense of Indigenous place, community, culture, language, history, politics, and the plurality of Indigenous being. There must be a nuanced comprehension of colonial impacts on Indigenous peoples and Indigenous resurgent actions. The researcher must know the history of research in Indigenous communities and why, as Linda Tuhiwai Smith (1999) writes, research was perceived as one of the most dirty words in Indigenous communities. It must be noted that the focus on decolonization is critical, but it must move beyond decolonizing perspectives to centering tribal knowledges.

Indigenous methodologies are grounded in one's own truth, story, and life. It is a grounding that is not divorced from community but rather assumes accountability to one's external world. This implies an understanding of reciprocity and respect from a deep ethical perspective.

Indigenous methodologies require an agility with story and an understanding of orality. Interpretations are understood as interpretations. Interpretations are grounded within an Indigenous worldview and community relations. Representations of knowledge allow for Indigenous symbology and ontology to emerge. Representations can be allegorical, metaphorical, holistic. They can include the written and spoken word, art, and the performative. However, such representation requires grounding in Indigenous ontology. It is an anchored representation.

Indigenous methodologies are imbued with an Indigenous relational sensibility. It is not add "talking circle" and stir. Reciprocity is a "gold standard," and the research gives back to community in a manner that meets community standards. Such research ought to create community with an understanding of the research's long-term impact on community. The authority of Indigenous research flowing from Indigenous methodologies is gained from a review and "nod" from the Indigenous communities it impacts.

As you can see, Indigenous methodologies demand a grounded backstory that involves Indigenous knowledge and relational systems. The beauty of this methodology is that it is for individuals who have lived their life in relationship to Indigenous peoples, culture, experiences, struggle, healing, and restitution. Indigenous methodologies are a viable research approach that offer a means to serve this experience within the research process.

I have often been asked if one who is not Indigenous can take up Indigenous methodologies. The more I learn, the more I recognize that it is not solely about identity—although I do not deny this is a consideration. However, it is more complex than one's lineage. What I have come to know is that the researcher's relational connections matter greatly. When budding researchers ask me whether they can take up Indigenous methodologies, I ask that they reflect upon their relationships with the Indigenous community. Often, if they are asking the question, they may not be best situated at this time in their lives. Indigenous methodologies are not an easy entry into Indigenous life without the requisite preparation that relational grounding demands. From this perspective, Indigenous methodologies are not for everyone. However, they are a choice for some—in particular Indigenous peoples—who have been made to believe that their cultural knowledge is unworthy, unsophisticated, and not rigorously intellectual.

For some concluding thoughts, I would like to reflect briefly upon the title of my talk for today, "Moving Forward, Pushing Back: Indigenous Methodologies in the Academy." If Indigenous methodologies are to maintain their integrity, we must continue to push back against the domesticating tendencies of Western intellectual tradition.

Indigenous methodologies are a legitimate qualitative inquiry approach. However, this remains contested within Western institutions. Recently, I had the fortune to be involved in a research project focusing on the experience of faculty members, both Indigenous and not, taking up Indigenous knowledges in their classrooms, research, and academic life. It was a research project guided by Indigenous principles. We were offered guidance by Cree elder Joseph Naytowhow. There were many rich findings from the report; however, there was one quote from an Indigenous faculty member that particularly resonated with me. When reflecting upon being an Indigenous faculty in the academy, this individual shared:

> I was shaped. I was formed. I was mentored. And I was tutored in my early career by Indigenous organizations and programming. But then I ended up

here, and I didn't realize being here would take me away from Indigenous programs and people.

(Kovach et al., 2015, pp. 70)

Western ideologies—be they conservative, liberal, or radical—all grapple with Indigenous knowledges and are a challenge to the autonomy of Indigenous scholarship. Nobody is off the hook. Casting an eye on Indigeniety, the Western gaze whatever its ideological motives sees a mirage necessary to soothe itself. Beyond this mirage lies a tribal knowing that sits deep in the lands. It is those lands, as stated earlier in the acknowledgement of this territory, that carry the memories of the ancestors through the stories of struggle for survival and identity (Acknowledging the Land, 2013).

Indigenous knowledges are distinct from Western knowledges. They are distinct because they arise from a different source, place, and history. Yet, while Indigenous knowledges are distinct from Western thought, there is not the desire to alienate ourselves from meaningful conversations that impact a shared world. Native American scholar Sandy Grande articulates the notion of a pedagogical and spiritual sovereignty that does not espouse separatism but rather advocates for "restorative process" of co-habitation with all the complexities that this implies. (Grande, 2004, pp. 57). For all of us who have been in relationships, we know that the complexities of co-habitation without losing oneself are not always easy street. It is work.

It has been over 20 years since I have been reflecting upon Indigenous knowledges in academic scholarship and research. During my early days I came across a quote by a Sioux leader, thinker, and activist. Over the years these words have run through my mind at least every couple of months—give or take. The quote is by Russell Means (1983), published in 1982. In commenting upon American Indians entering university and "other European institutions," he said,

> If you are there to learn to resist the oppressor in accordance with your traditional ways, so be it. I don't know how you manage to combine the two, but perhaps you will succeed. But retain your sense of reality. Beware of coming to believe the Euro world now offers solutions to the problems it confronts us with.

(pp. 32)

He went on to say, "Draw your strength from who you are" (pp. 32). In reflecting upon recent resurgence within Indigenous country, Adam J. Barker, a self-identified settler-Canadian author, reflected upon the global Indigenous movement *Idle No More* and Indigenous activism. He had this to say: "If Idle No More has demonstrated anything, it is that Indigenous peoples will not cease pursuing decolonisation, nationhood, and social change because that is the condition and effect of their existence" (2014, pp.18). He went on to quote Anishinaabe activist Leanne

Simpson as getting to point of the matter: "Simpson's phrase explains it best when she says, 'For me, living as a Nishnaabekwe is a deliberate act—a direct act of resurgence, a direct act of sovereignty' (2014)" (pp. 18). Pushing back against domesticating norms of Western intellectual tradition requires vigilance and clarity. Russell Means's words re-enter my consciousness: "Retain your sense of reality." "Draw your strength from who you are."

What will qualitative inquiry look like in the next decade? Qualitative inquiry will not only include but will be influenced by Indigenous methodologies. To dismiss Indigenous methodologies will be to dismiss Indigenous knowledges, and that is nothing less than neo-colonialism. We will know that we are there when we consistently expect all researchers to respond to these three questions: How has your research contributed to knowledge? How has your research created community? How has your research shown care for the land upon which our grandchildren will live? I hope that I have shared enough about Indigenous methodologies to entice further conversation in the ongoing sessions and networking of the Congress. There are a number of sessions on Indigenous qualitative inquiry. If I understand correctly, there are at least 30 presentations that are associated with the Indigenous Inquiries Circle. They are open to all conference participants.

In closing, earlier this spring I was contemplating Tewa scholar Alfonso Ortiz's writing in his 1969 book *The Tewa World—Space, Time, Being and Becoming in a Pueblo Society*. This book is one of the first contemporary academic writings on Indigenous knowledges. He begins chapter 2 with a Tewa prayer. To me it is about place, belonging, and ultimately respect and responsibility. It is a prayer for the Tewa people. I think they are good words for us all.

> Within and around the earth,
> within and around the hills,
> within and around the mountains,
> your authority returns to you.
> *Ekosi*
> *Hai, Hai*

(p. 13)

Note

1 This chapter was presented as a keynote address to the eleventh annual International Congress of Qualitative Inquiry, May 2015.

References

Acknowledging the Land. (2013). C. Campbell, H. Montgomery, & H. Ritenburg (guest eds.), *International Review of Qualitative Research Journal. Indigenous Inquiries Special Edition*, 6(4). Walnut Creek: CA. Left Coast Press.

Anderson, A. (2007). Aboriginal Population Trends. *The Encyclopedia of Saskatchewan* (2006 ed.). Retrieved from http://esask.uregina.ca/entry/aboriginal_population_trends.html.

Barker, A.J. (2014). 'A Direct Act of Resurgence, a Direct Act of Sovereignty': Reflections on Idle No More, Indigenous Activism, and Canadian Settler Colonialism. *Globalizations, 12*(1), 1–20. doi.org/10.1080/14747731.2014.971531.

Bird-David, N. (1999). "Animism" Revisited—Personhood, Environment, and Relational Epistemology. *Current Anthropology, 40*, 67–91.

Denzin, N. (2015, May 20–23). Welcome from the Director. *Eleventh International Congress of Qualitative Inquiry*. University of Illinois at Urbana-Champaign.

Grande, S. (2004). *Red Pedagogy—Native American Social and Political Thought*. Lanham, MD: Rowman & Littlefield.

Hutchinson, B. (2015, May 8). UBC Student Writes 52,438 Word Architecture Dissertation With No Punctuation—Not Everyone Loved It. *National Post*. Retrieved from http://news.nationalpost.com/news/canada/ubc-student-writes-52438-word-architecture-dissertation-with-no-punctuation-not-everyone-loved-it.

Kovach, M., Carriere, J., Montgomery H., Barrett, M.J., & Gilles, C. (2015). *Indigenous Presence: Experiencing and Envisioning Indigenous Knowledges Within Selected Sites of Education and Social Work*. Retrieved from http://www.usask.ca/education/profiles/kovach/Indigenous-Presence-2014-Kovach-M-et-al.pdf.

Means, R. (1983). The Same Old Song. In W. Churchill (Eds.), *Marxism and Native Americans* (pp. 19–33). Boston: Southend Press.

Ortiz, A. (1969). *The Tewa World—Space, Time, Being and Becoming in a Pueblo Society*. Chicago: University of Chicago Press.

Saskatchewan School Boards Association. (2009). *A Summary of Saskatchewan Board of Education Initiatives for Aboriginal Employment and Student Success* (Research Report #09–04). Retrieved from http://www.saskschoolboards.ca/old/ResearchAndDevelopment/ResearchReports/IndianAndMetisEducation/09-04.pdf.

Statistics Canada. (2010). *Growth Rate (%) Between 1996 and 2006, by Aboriginal Identity*. Retrieved from http://www.statcan.gc.ca/pub/89–645-x/2010001/c-g/c-g002-eng.htm.

Stewart, P. (2015). *Indigenous Architecture Through Indigenous Knowledge: Dim sagalts'apkw nisin [Together We Build a Village]*. (Unpublished doctoral dissertation). Interdisciplinary Studies. University of British Columbia, Vancouver, British Columbia.

Tuhiwai Smith, L. (1999). *Decolonizing Methodologies—Research and Indigenous Peoples* (1st ed.). London: Zed Books.

Wilson, S. (2001). What Is an Indigenous Research Methodology? *Journal of Native Education, 25*(2), 175–179.

Wilson, S. (2008). *Research Is Ceremony—Indigenous Research Methods*. Winnipeg: Fernwood Press.

3

THE POWER OF STORIES AND THE POTENTIAL OF THEORIZING FOR SOCIAL JUSTICE STUDIES

Kathy Charmaz

Before considering the power of stories and the potential of theorizing, I begin with a caveat and tell a story. Treat my words as provisional, not as prescriptive. Take what I say as a source of comparison to think about methods and interrogate them and to reach beyond our methods of today to create the methods for tomorrow.

Our methods form a silent frame that shapes our research. It's time to break open our methodological frames as many of you have done in the past. I aim to take the conversation further. When I talk about methods, I include how we interpret the stories we hear and events we see as well as how we gather our research participants' stories. Any method needs to be critically examined.

Not all methods fit the situations we study. Not all methods fit the worlds to which our research participants belong. Any set of ideas, any method, must be located in time, place, and situation. Our methods and forms of analysis are located in the conditions of their production, and mine, grounded theory, is no exception. I have noted earlier that Barney Glaser and Anselm Strauss developed grounded theory during a time of unquestioned capitalism, which informed the method (Charmaz, 2014a, 2014b). Our methods do not stand outside the structures in which we live. The structures in which we construct our methods and conduct our research extend their reach into our taken-for-granted ways of thinking about methods and using them.

Interview Stories and Stories About Interviewing: Critiques of the Method

Storied Interviews

To start our discussion, consider Carla's story from an interview about having serious illnesses.[1] At 54, Carla had managed to create a successful business, despite struggling with fatigue and pain from fibromyalgia throughout her adult years. While establishing her business, she raised two children on her own. She was the oldest of five children, and her parents had taught her that her role was to take care of other family members. When Carla was 12, her baby brother was born, and she essentially raised him. She had remained close to her brother since then. Carla began her story of what had happened during the past few years:

> I was making a lot of money and doing really well and we decided to go into business together as partners, 50/50. When I got diagnosed with cancer, he was building a million dollar home [within a few years real estate rose astronomically in her area; the house would now be 4 to 6 million]. He had just gotten married, and I performed the wedding. He had married my doctor, who was my family practitioner. And when I was diagnosed with cancer they got angry at me, the two of them because it wasn't—it was ill-timed and it wasn't convenient for them and I was the sales person. I was the one that brought in all the money: they were building this million dollar house, and how dare I get cancer?

Carla had thought that she would just continue working while having her treatments and promised to do so. But she became very ill. Carla's relationship with her brother deteriorated, and so did the business arrangement. She recounted the unfolding events:

> He decided I shouldn't get any money any more so I had to borrow to live from someone else and then I went to a meeting with my brother. Ostensibly I thought we were going to get some kind of written partnership agreement because we didn't have one and I find out that he wanted to take the whole business from me. So then I had to get an attorney. So now I had drains 'cause I had a second mastectomy. I had drains coming out of my breasts and I was sick as a dog. And I was bald, and I'd already been through eight rounds of chemotherapy and 40 some odd rounds of radiation, and I was with lawyer and he [her brother] was trying to take everything away from me, and in the business bracket was really all mine.

Carla told a story of broken trust, shattered bonds, a fractured family, and lost hopes, dreams, and purpose—and of injustice. It's a particular type of injustice that occurs in and disrupts routine everyday life. I call it liminal injustice.

People who experience liminal injustice find themselves in an ambiguous place between the known past and an unsettled future. They lack the anchors of familiar roles and shared understandings. The liminal injustice that Carla experienced often develops between warring spouses whose interactions are filled with ambiguity and ambivalence about rights, fairness, and wrongdoing. Liminal injustice elicits unsettling feelings as awareness of unfair treatment surfaces. It may be shouted in anger or shrouded in silence, shame, and self-blame.

Experiencing liminal injustice leads to searching the past to understand the present. One older man was in the midst of a nasty divorce from his second wife when he had a massive heart attack. He awoke in the hospital to find her with pen in hand shoving her lawyer's version of their property settlement in his face. He tried to treat the incident as a hilarious testimony to her character and pondered, "What else can you do but laugh? Have another heart attack? Why did I ever marry her?" Throughout the interview, he repeated the question, "Why did I ever marry *her?*"

For Carla, questions arose about what family meant during troubles and turmoil. Her situation also caused her to question her moral value and personal significance to members of her family—and to herself. Carla was losing more than her health. She was losing the self that she had known and valued and her place in her family. Carla said her father and his wife downplayed the seriousness of her condition and "couldn't deal with it." Nor could her teenage son who added to her distress by "acting out." Carla not only said her family ignored the seriousness of her condition during this harrowing and continuing life-threatening illness, but she also talked of suffering from her brother's barrage of abusive emails, legal threats, and continued financial manipulations—all from the brother she raised and loved the most. Carla believed that her father should have supported her and intervened with her brother. But she discovered her father and his wife did not want to get involved. Carla said:

> I felt really sad; I felt abandoned; I felt let down. I felt worthless. I felt unloved. I felt sometimes like I didn't want to live, that death would be more merciful, because in addition to feeling physically crappy, I felt emotionally awful. And so in all that it was real hard for me to stay sort of conscious spiritually, and I was like losing my whole spirit and I had a lot of anger.

Meanwhile, with the exception of her daughter's support, Carla was left alone to deal with having metastatic cancer and the prospect of a foreshortened life. She mentioned, "Another problem I have with my oncologist because she believes that once you metastasize you're history . . ."

Critiques of Interviews and Interviewing

What does Carla's story tell us about qualitative methods? How might it help us to reflect upon the methods we use? You may wonder why I am treating Carla's tale as given when it is an interview account. What purposes do interview stories serve? Carla told a poignant story of pain and sorrow about loss—loss of connection, loss of health, and loss of love. Is it true? Is Carla's story an artifact of the interview?

Criticisms of interviewing abound. Ethnographers, discourse researchers, and conversational analysts (Atkinson & Silverman, 1997; Miczo, 2003) raise trenchant objections to interview methods. They might question the veracity of Carla's story and her purposes for what she tells and how she tells it. Here are a few of the litany of criticisms wielded against interview stories:

- Interviews produce contrived data
- Interviews are performed retrospective accounts
- Interview accounts justify past behavior
- Interviewees engage in impression management
- Interviewing assumes a hierarchical relationship
- Interviewing is "too easy, too obvious, too little studied"—and leads to poor research (Potter & Hepburn, 2012, p. 555)

Such criticisms comprise the list of obvious acknowledged concerns. These criticisms often assume research should seek and can provide a reproduction of reality. From this perspective, interviews do not elicit accurate accounts. Such criticisms also assume one-shot interviews between two strangers. That may not be the case. A formal interview may follow a lengthy relationship between two people who are well known to each other. Some interview studies consist of more than one interviewer and more than one research participant. Yes, like the content of many ordinary conversations, interview stories may justify past behavior. Also like ordinary conversations, research participants' efforts to make a particular impression may be more or less explicit—or not intended at all.

Most qualitative interviewers aim to create an egalitarian rather than a hierarchical relationship. Whether this goal is successful depends on the topic, context, social statuses of the researcher and participant, and the specific research situation. Consistent with Potter and Hepburn's (2012) comment that interviewing is too little studied, their assertion that interviewing leads to poor research also needs to be put to empirical test.

In contrast to the criticisms above, the following concerns are somewhat less discernible and less discussed:

- Interviewers may lack knowledge of their participants' worlds
- Interviewing may not fit the research question

Gaining intimate familiarity with the participants' world can require concerted effort that an interview study may preclude. Interviewers who lack knowledge of their participants' specialized terms likely miss implicit meanings or, worse, mistakenly assume disparate meanings are shared. Increasingly, researchers need to understand the participants' goals, concerns, and daily life before they can construct a useful interview guide. Researchers who study complex business settings or technological situations, for example, need to be familiar with them before conducting interviews. Furthermore, a research design based on one interview per participant does not fit research questions for which lengthy researcher-participant relationships are prerequisite. Two other criticisms need to be brought into focus.

- Interviews rely on talk, neglect silences
- Interviews are predicated on unearned trust

These criticisms merit further discussion in the methods literature. To me, reliance on talk and unearned trust are more significant concerns. Reliance on talk limits or obscures attention to context. This criticism extends beyond interviewing; it also pertains to the methods of vocal critics of interviewing. Reliance on talk can erase significant experiences, conceal unstated and unrecognized assumptions, and suppress meanings of silence. Unearned trust raises questions about research ethics and methodological goals. A common theme in the literature promotes gaining trust and rapport to elicit research participants' personal views and hidden experiences. Such purposes hint of manipulation. Why should our participants trust us?

Methods talk includes much discussion about building rapport and gaining trust—as a means of obtaining data (see, for example, Fontana & Prokos 2007; Grinyer & Thomas 2012; King & Horrocks 2010). But this discussion overlooks examining what trust means to the participants and who merits having it.

When potential research participants believe talking about the research topic could be harmful to them, interviewing is unlikely to be a useful method. Their resistance to being interviewed intensifies. During an interview, they may reveal very little about themselves and the topic (Kusow 2003). Unearned trust elicits silence, not stories of lived experience.

Robert Garot (2013) spent almost six months as a participant observer at a trade union office that provided services to African immigrants in Tuscany. He next aimed to conduct interviews with the immigrants, but his potential research participants routinely refused to be interviewed. Others who had agreed to an interview decided against it when Garot asked them to sign the consent form. His request raised their fears that he was a police spy. One astute young man carefully reviewed the interview questions before beginning. Garot writes:

> He didn't like the question "Did you need help from anyone to find work," and demanded, "Why do you want to know that?" "I want to understand your experiences," I said. "Why you wanna understand my experiences?" I found myself telling him why I went to school, how long I was in school ("Why you in school so long?"). I pointed to the bookstore behind him, and told him I wanted to write a book, "like those." We eventually agreed that I would take notes as he talked.
>
> *(para. 13)*

Confronting what unearned trust means in social justice research can elicit the researcher's disquieting realizations and awareness of taken-for-granted privileges and dubious alliances. Garot realized that these men saw his questioning as reproducing colonial subjugation. He found himself interpreting for the police and being manipulated by them to extend the Italian state's oppression of immigrants. Garot states that "as ethnographers, we are their [police] auxiliaries. Despite whatever our intentions, ethnography is a form of surveillance, often deeply complicit in the police state" (para. 21).

Ethnographers constantly watch. But who helps them focus their gaze matters. When researchers rely exclusively on interviews, they may gain access to research participants from authorities who preselect the interviewees. In turn, the selected individuals may feel pressured to participate and to present a perspective they may not endorse. In such situations, the problems of unearned trust likely increase. Subsequently, researchers' understanding of their respective participants' worlds likely decrease.

As qualitative researchers, we must struggle to understand and interpret the meanings, experiences, and actions of the people we study and the stories they tell. Interview stories may reveal troubling personal experiences, whether our participants have suffered profound injustice or whether they are perpetrators of injustice.

Critics of interviewing highlight its potential limitations and hazards. These critics seldom acknowledge the strengths of the method. When we think about Carla's interview story, what does it suggest? Might it mean something more than a calculated performance or justification for *her* actions toward her brother? Are there unacknowledged benefits of interviewing? What do critics of intensive interviewing miss? The power of face-to-face interaction (Charmaz 2014a, 2015). What can result from this interaction?

- Connection
- Reflection
- Disclosure
- Intimacy
- *Emergence*

Intensive interviews foster an intimate connection between interviewer and the research participant(s). An interview can create the time and space for reflection. The experience of being interviewed can validate that participants' stories matter and are worthy of consideration. A participant's reflections during an interview may spawn new realizations and interpretations of the past. Hence interviews can be sites of emergent reconstruction of meaning (Conlon et al., 2015). Interviews *are* emergent interactions; they are embodied interactions that occur in specific situations and times (Ellingson 2012; Ezzy 2010). Interviews give us one window for grappling with and grasping the significance of our participants' stories.

Reconstructing Qualitative Inquiry

Qualitative inquiry is part art, part science. Qualitative researchers have long demonstrated the power of stories. We have excelled at telling stories about the lives of individuals, including our own. Theorizing in qualitative research has been less developed. Storytelling and theorizing may seem to represent two distinct forms of qualitative inquiry that reside at opposite ends of a continuum, art and science.[2] Our research stories document individuals' troubles and triumphs. We can build on their stories to create theoretical analyses of them that tell a collective story. We have applied earlier theories to stories with success, but the potential of fresh theorizing has yet to be realized.

To construct *one* new form of qualitative inquiry, I return to an established methodology: grounded theory. But I do so informed by epistemological questions and methodological innovations that occurred over the past five decades. I advocate establishing greater mutual appreciation of our varied methodological approaches and for more integration of various methods. Methodological purism can stifle innovation; methodological integration may enhance it.

For those of you who are new to qualitative inquiry or to grounded theory, here is a short definition of grounded theory: Grounded theory is a systematic method of inquiry that begins with inductive data, moves back and forth between collecting and analyzing data, relies on comparative methods, builds checks into the research process, and aims to construct theory.

Interrogating What We Do and How We Do It

Part of reconstructing qualitative inquiry means looking at what we do, why we do it, and how we do it. International and Indigenous researchers criticize the Anglo–North American dominance in qualitative inquiry (see, for example, Alasuutari, 2004; Hsiung, 2015; Kovach, 2009; Smith, 1999, 2005). They show how Anglo–North American qualitative methods and their fundamental assumptions do not always easily cross borders to other parts of the world. To me, a major problem is that qualitative methods and perspectives reproduce the individualism underlying Anglo–North American cultures.

Assuming individualism as a perspective leads to methodological individualism.[3] My work is not exempt from this problem. As a social psychologist, my perspective assumes focusing on the individual. More generally, individualism underlies our methods and often our renderings of the experiences of the people we study. Their stories, their experiences, often differ from our own. Grasping participants' meanings and experiences requires openness and diligence and an awareness of context and culture that we may lack. Many of us study people who have suffered profound distress, disruption, and disappointment. Interpreting their stories requires humility, caring, and attention to silences.

On another level, we need to lay open *why* we do what we do. I see considerable careerism sparking methodological moves and trends. Calls to abandon traditional qualitative methods may advance careers more than qualitative inquiry. Rather than abandoning earlier methods, I call for appreciating and building on them. Calling for appreciation includes taking a fresh look at our own methods with humor and humility. If we lack either humor or humility, Johnny Saldaña (2014) prods us by shooting sharp arrows our way. In his recent critique in *Qualitative Inquiry*, he does not simply criticize method. Instead, he criticizes qualitative researchers from the perspective of his working-class origins. He confronts the upper-middle-class dominance pervading qualitative methods and the reproduction of power to define them in esoteric academic terms. Saldaña punctures methodological pretensions and pontifications. He contends:

- If you call yourself a "post-*anything*," you need to bring it down a notch.
- If you teach a lot 'bout theory, but haven't come up with any original theory theories of your own, you need to bring it down a notch.

(p. 979)

My favorite among Saldaña's array of charges:

- If you're a professor and really don't want your students to read this article, you [*really*] need to bring it down a notch.

(p. 980)

Saldaña has more criticisms. I think there's one at least one for each of us. It's quite possible that you, like me, agree with a number of the things that Johnny says—*except those that apply to our particular method and priorities.* As he states:

- If you say you're usin' grounded theory, but don't have a core category, you need to bring it down a notch.
- If you think that anythin' is "undertheorized," you need to bring it down a notch.

(p. 979)

I don't agree with either of his pronouncements here. You can use grounded theory strategies to the extent that fits your research purpose, as long as you have a solid grasp of the method and own what you do with it. And, yes, much of qualitative research *is* undertheorized. By this term, I mean studies that only provide a descriptive synthesis or merely show how earlier theories illuminate the data. Such renderings of qualitative data differ from creating new conceptualizations of studied life.

We can construct new ideas about the stories we gather, and grounded theory is one approach that fosters analytic development. It also is a useful toolkit for social justice studies. Of major importance here, grounded theory provides explicit tools for identifying and analyzing processes. It also aids in explicating research participants' implicit meanings and actions. This method enables us to not only increase the theoretical significance of our analyses but also acknowledge the complexity of the empirical world. Social justice researchers who study processes and address empirical complexity can produce nuanced, persuasive reports.

Coding Qualitative Data?

Coding? I'm all for it. But what kind of coding? Coding is a way of getting to the fundamentals to work with the data and define what stories suggest. Coding can accomplish more than data reduction or thematic synthesis. Rather, coding can break the data open to view it anew. In keeping with Saldaña's (2014) logic, coding is "bringing data down a notch."[4] Coding means getting to the core of the data, defining their foundations, and immersing oneself in these data.

Critics of coding (Brinkmann, 2014; St. Pierre & Jackson, 2014) view it as a time-consuming endeavor that yields trivial results. True, much coding is mundane and generates trite descriptions. I regret that earlier forms of grounded theory became known for being procedural and prescriptive, particularly about coding data. Yet grounded theory can offer much more. We can use it as flexible guidelines rather than prescriptive rules. We North Americans have a tendency to throw out what is useful as well as what doesn't work or might be improved. We also tend to give methods a superficial appraisal without necessarily grappling with using them.

Grounded-theory coding is a way of engaging with the data, of taking a closer, fresh look at studied life. This type of coding is a heuristic device that prompts the researcher to be active in the research process. Early coding in grounded theory involves an embodied process in which the researcher is steadily writing or typing and thinking. There's something kinesthetic about this involvement that pushes the researcher forward. The actions involved in continuous writing or typing and thinking foster delving into the data and building analytic momentum. Active involvement in coding opens possibilities for the unexpected to occur.

Coding can be magical rather than merely mechanical. Coding links the researcher to the story. It links the data to the analysis. Grounded theory coding is one way to remain thoroughly empirical while taking the stories we hear further into analysis. Coding gives us an initial step into theorizing. Coding is a way to help us to be more reflexive about our analyses. In my view, we cannot code as if we are identifying some objective external phenomenon. Rather, we need to trouble our codes and how we arrive at them.

Using Grounded Theory in Social Justice Research

Social justice studies may seem to require practical, concrete research with immediate applications. In contrast, I contend that theorizing qualitative data can make important contributions to social justice research. Qualitative researchers who explicitly direct their work toward social justice may find it useful to examine the significance of the material world, language, time, agency and constraint, as well as implicit meanings and tangible actions.

Addressing these areas is part of a lengthy tradition among scholars of pragmatist philosophy and its sociological descendent, symbolic interactionism. I have long advocated attending to language, symbols, unstated meanings, and experiences that participants treat as beyond words (Charmaz, 1991, 2006, 2014b). I suggest here how several of these emphases inform theorizing in two studies that arose from social justice concerns.

First, Jason Wasserman and Jeffrey Michael Clair (2010) began with a grounded theory ethnography that they chronicled in their book *At Home on the Street*, and they later built on their ethnographic knowledge in a sophisticated rhetorical analysis, "The Insufficiency of Fairness" (2013). This analysis emerged from a close study of the language and meanings that service organizations invoked to justify providing services to the homeless. Wasserman and Clair argue that service providers decided who could receive service from a conception of fairness rooted in an economic model of a fair exchange between providers and homeless people. The providers offered help *if* homeless people declared themselves needing the kind of treatment given in the specific shelter. When discussing his research with John Davis (2010), Wasserman said:

> It seemed the shelters dealt with addiction and mental illness almost exclusively. That's great if that's your problem, but alienating if it's not. One thing nearly all homeless people do want is jobs. They don't want treatment or even meals. But they will work and they will push and shove to get a job.
> *(in Davis, 2010)*

Wasserman and Clair argue that the logic of efficient production demands a focus on homeless individuals that narrow them down to those personal characteristics such as alcoholism or mental illness that are essential to the provided treatment. That is, the homeless are transformed from people into cases. Any qualities of a person that are peripheral to the disease for which he or she is being treated not only are extraneous but, moreover, oppose efficiency (Wasserman & Clair, 2013, pp. 179–180). Essentially, Wasserman and Clair challenge the assumptions on which service providers manufacture assembly-line social justice on their terms.[5]

Many qualitative researchers study disadvantaged people and want to help change their situations. If so, starting research *with* (not on or about) these people and their concerns moves our studies toward social justice. We can take Wasserman and Clair's (2011) stance and apply it to social justice studies more broadly. They argue that we must discard our taken-for-granted beliefs about the "problem" and how to solve it. Taking this stance can lead us to relinquish assumptions that a specific problem requires solutions that service providers and the public assume (such as when homeless people are defined as the problem).

Second, in their study of social movements and collective actions, David Snow and Dana Moss tell a decidedly analytic story with practical implications for social justice activists. Snow and Moss (2014) delineate the significance of ambiguous moments for directing and redirecting events during a social movement. They used grounded theory as a fine-meshed net to catch elusive strands of meaning in descriptions and stories in multiple sources, including their own ethnographic studies, firsthand participant accounts, published resources, and government documents. Snow and Moss coded and compared these materials and then developed and checked their emergent categories. Their subsequent analysis explains relationships between meaning and action, between beliefs and behavior.

Through using grounded theory strategies, Snow and Moss arrived at focusing on spontaneity in social movements and on its links between time and action. Based on their observations, Snow and Moss argue that spontaneous action involves cognition—thinking—but it is compressed in time when compared with prior deliberation. Thinking is not absent. Spontaneous actions then spur collective actions.

Snow and Moss lay out four conditions for a theory of spontaneity in social and protest movements:

(1) non-hierarchical movements,
(2) ambiguous moments and events when scripted behavior breaks down, is disrupted, or dissolves,
(3) behavioral/emotional priming and framing when recent prior sentiments and experiences inform and frame spontaneous actions, and
(4) ecological/spatial contexts and constraints.

Snow recounts the story of how he had seized on an ambiguous moment at a 1970 University of Akron protest over the then recent killing of four protesters at nearby Kent State University. During an awkward pause, no speaker came forward, and the crowd did not seem to know what to do next. Snow yelled, "Strike! Strike! Shut it down!" (Snow & Moss, 2014, p. 1132) and sparked the crowd's actions. They echoed his slogan and marched to the administrative building.

By recognizing the conditions and contingencies involved in emergent protests, social movement leaders, like Snow, can seize ambiguous moments to construct effective actions. Through using grounded theory strategies, we, too, can analyze our stories to define the conditions for enacting change.

Moving Qualitative Social Justice Forward: Studying Power and Suffering

Last, I wish to address two understudied areas concerning social justice: power and suffering. We need to conduct studies of the powerful, of people with whom we do not agree. We need to know how they implement and maintain power as well as what it means to be subject to it. Studying the powerful can mean developing new methods, finding ways to get information kept secret or obscured—such as tucked away in incomprehensible organizational reports and budgets. Studying the powerful means rethinking how we gather stories and reexamining the empathetic approach that characterizes much social science interviewing and ethnography.

Studying the exercise of power may require new approaches to qualitative inquiry. I should note that studying the powerful is not easy and can be dangerous. A few weeks ago, a former fellow master's student at San Francisco State University contacted me. We caught up on some of our mutual acquaintances. One of our classmates had gone to law school after his degree in sociology. Over the years he had maintained his sociological curiosity and sense of social justice. It had led him to conducting investigative research that threatened to expose some powerful figures. Before publicizing his findings, he died in a mysterious one-car accident in an isolated mountainous part of California. His friends attribute his untimely death to the research he was doing.

In turning to suffering as a topic of inquiry, I conclude this chapter with a brief observation about studying suffering and with a story. Social scientists, particularly those in my field, sociology, have not yet developed a robust research literature on suffering. Gareth Williams (2006) may clarify why in his review essay, "Suffering Sociologists and the Sociology of Suffering." He distinguishes between writing that is *informed by* suffering and writing *about* suffering. Stories of suffering may provide a context from which researchers pursue other topics. Many researchers address stories *informed by* suffering; few researchers write *about* suffering. Janice Morse and her colleagues (see, for example, Morse & Penrod [1999] and Kumar Ravi Priya [2010]) are notable exceptions, and they are not sociologists. Williams's distinction suggests that addressing suffering may provide a lens on inequality and injustice. Yet he holds an ambivalent view of suffering that many academics share.

> If the concept of suffering helps us to make more visible the connections between social and economic change and the fabric of everyday life, experiences of poverty, homelessness and incapacity, and to write about them more powerfully then it seems to me that we should welcome it. If it deflects us into the vortex of subjectivity, then it seems to me that we are engaging with experiences that are better dealt with by poetry.
>
> *(2006, p. 41)*

I disagree.

Through studying suffering and writing about it, we can link the subjective to the social and better understand both. Moreover, we may gain an understanding of fundamental dimensions of human existence. Few can escape suffering. Yet its meaning draws on what occurred in the past and what the future portends as well as on present experience. Past, present, and future are all socially situated. As our research participants tell us their stories, they may teach us not only about suffering but also how it is imbedded in the social conditions of their lives.

Rosanna tells a story of her life with illness and speaks of suffering. Rosanna attributed her onset of chronic fatigue syndrome after having breast implants 16 years before at age 27. At that time, she held a fast-paced position in sales in the high-tech industry. She described her job as being an extremely stressful dawn-past-dusk position that entailed keeping the company's complex financial accounts, supervising the work of nine managers, and filling in for employees who quit or were fired:

> I never felt like I recovered from the anesthesia, uhh, but I don't know if that's what it was. . . . I just kept feeling like I wasn't well, and umm, it continued and it got worse and worse and worse, umm, mainly the heavy fatigue, I was forgetting—cognitive. . . . I was forgetting everything left and right and I was so exhausted I was coming in to work later and later and later.

Rosanna received her breast implants at a time when the manufacturers were hiding known risks. Like many people with invisible illnesses, Rosanna had to fight to be taken seriously by physicians as well as friends and co-workers despite her constant symptoms, including cardiac arrhythmias (see also Dumit, 2006). One physician after another told her she looked fine and her blood work was normal. Eventually she went to a doctor a girlfriend had recommended because he took the time to diagnose her own elusive condition. This doctor also told Rosanna she was all right, but she refused to accept his opinion:

> I have makeup and I'm dressed up and I walk in and you [the doctor] look at me and you're like "Oh, you look fine." You know but inside I felt like somebody was just tearing my body apart, I had no energy and I couldn't remember anything and I couldn't think straight. So, I'm like, "Look at me I'm dying," that's what it felt like. I was dying and you know, nobody was gonna find out 'til it was too late and then I was gonna croak. So, I just—I got mad and I pounded my fists on his desk and I looked at him and said, "If you can't find out what I've got, cause I know I look fine but I'm not, I'll go to somebody else who will!" I kind of like challenged him [laughs] and his male ego, and sure enough I don't know if that did it, but he pursued, even though my blood work looked fine.

This doctor first diagnosed her as having the Epstein-Bar virus. Later she was also diagnosed with having a virus similar to HIV that caused enormous fatigue, cognitive dysfunction, myalgia, and heart symptoms. Rosanna lost her health, her job, and her credibility. Somehow she qualified for disability and at the time of the interview lived an anonymous life in a rented room in a rural area far from her earlier life. It was all she could afford. She lived a life of imposed silence without connection or care. Rosanna said of suffering:

> Nobody escapes it and we create a lot of our own suffering by, umm, mis-interpreting what will make us happy. Religious institutions help create a lot of suffering unnecessarily. So, umm, basically I've been in the last—since I've been sick—I've also been deconditioning myself and letting go of so many untruths, things that were fed to me, and that's alleviating a lot of suffering and a lot of control of things that were controlling me. There's been a lot of pain and suffering, emotional pain and suffering, I still have emotional pain and suffering. What the illness did, was take me into a—a depth of my being that I wasn't familiar with. So, um, that's where I've been getting my strength from, as well as, I mean it's really made me into understanding, umm, well it's got me acquainted with self-hate, got me acquainted with self-love, and how to recognize it.
>
> For me what I think to do is to not push away, to make my feelings OK, whatever they are, and allow them expression because they're there and they want to be heard they want some acknowledgement and really what it's all down to is just myself wants love, my attention is love, my acceptance is love and you know, umm, if I'm suffering it's my being talking to me, wanting to tell me something.

So the moral of my story is for you to tell your stories. Think about being open to methods you haven't used, consider creating new methods, and look for forms of injustice in the stories you hear. And while you think and work, listen to the poetry as ordinary people tell you stories of their lives.

Acknowledgments

This chapter is an expanded version of a 2015 keynote address for the International Congress of Qualitative Inquiry. I greatly appreciated the honor of the invitation to give the address and thank Norman Denzin, Michael Giardina, James Salvo, Nathalie Tiberghien, and the members of the organizing committee for the opportunity. Thanks are also due to the following members of the Sonoma State University Faculty Writing Program for their comments on an earlier version of the chapter: Karen Grady, Diana Grant, Elizabeth Joniak-Grant, Lauren Morimoto, and Kurt Sollanek.

Notes

1 My comments on interviewing focus on intensive interviews in which the research participant has considerable experience concerning the topic and typically a specific stance on it.

2 The usual distinction is to juxtapose qualitative research against quantitative research, the former as art, the latter as science. However, a range of definitions between art and science also is evident in qualitative inquiry.

3 I use the concept "methodological individualism" to highlight the focus on individuals in qualitative inquiry and emphasis on the individual level of analysis without excavating the structural contexts and collective ideologies on which the particular individual level of analysis rests. The concept of methodological individualism commands a lengthy literature including Weberian (Weber, 1968) prescriptions to study individual actions, Marxist critiques and debates (e.g., Elster, 1982; Weldes, 1989), and assumptions undergirding rational choice theories, game theory, and microeconomics.

4 I thank Elizabeth Joniak-Grant for explicating the connection between coding and Johnny Saldaña's logic.

5 I am indebted to Diana Grant for the concept of assembly-line social justice.

References

Alasuutari, Pertti. 2004. The globalization of qualitative research. In *Qualitative Research Practice* (pp. 595–608), Giampietro Gobo, Clive Seale, Jaber F. Gubrium, and David Silverman eds. Thousand Oaks, CA: Sage.

Atkinson, Paul, and Silverman, David. 1997. Kundera's immortality: The interview society and the invention of the self. *Qualitative Inquiry* 3, 3: 304–325.

Brinkmann, Svend. 2014. Doing without data. *Qualitative Inquiry* 20, 6: 720–725.

Charmaz, Kathy. 2015. Teaching theory construction with initial grounded theory tools: A reflection on lessons and learning. *Qualitative Health Research* 25, 12: 1610–1622.

Charmaz, Kathy. 2014a. *Constructing grounded theory 2nd ed.* London: Sage.

Charmaz, K. 2014b. Grounded theory in global perspective: Reviews by international researchers. *Qualitative Inquiry* 20, 9: 1074–1084.

Charmaz, Kathy. 2006. *Constructing grounded theory: A practical guide through qualitative analysis.* London: Sage.

Charmaz, Kathy. 1991. *Good days, bad days: The self in chronic illness and time.* New Brunswick, NJ: Rutgers University Press.

Conlon, Catherine, Carney, Glemma, Timonen, Virpi, & Scharf, Thomas. 2015. 'Emergent reconstruction' in grounded theory: Learning from team-based interview research. *Qualitative Research* 15, 1: 39–56.

Davis, John. 2010. On the streets: Why homeless people refuse shelter. *Texas Tech Today.* January 22.

Dumit, Joseph. 2006. Illnesses you have to fight to get: Facts as forces in uncertain, emergent illnesses. *Social Science & Medicine* 62, 3: 577–590.

Ellingson, Laura. 2012. Interview as embodied communication. In *Handbook of Interview Research 2nd ed.* (pp. 525–539), Jaber F. Gubrium, James A. Holstein, Amir B. Marvasti, and Karyn D. Marvasti eds. Thousand Oaks, CA: Sage.

Elster, Jon. 1982. The case for methodological individualism. *Theory and Society* 11, 4: 453–482.

Ezzy, Douglas. 2010. Qualitative interviewing as an embodied emotional performance. *Qualitative Inquiry* 16, 3: 163–170.

Fontana, Andrea, and Prokos, Anastasia H. 2007. *The interview.* Walnut Creek, CA: Left Coast Press.

Garot, Robert. 2013. The psycho-affective echoes of colonialism in fieldwork relations [21 paragraphs]. Forum Qualitative Sozialforschung / Forum: Qualitative Social Research, 15, 1, Art. 12, http://nbn-resolving.de/urn:nbn:de:0114-fqs1401125.

Grinyer, Anne, and Thomas, Carol. 2012. The value of interviewing on multiple occasions or longitudinally. In *Handbook of Interview Research 2nd ed.* (pp. 219–230), Jaber F. Gubrium, James A. Holstein, Amir B. Marvasti, and Karyn D. Marvasti eds. Thousand Oaks, CA: Sage.

Hsiung, Ping-Chun. 2015. Doing (critical) qualitative research in China in a global era. *International Sociology 30*, 1: 86–102.

King, Nigel, and Horrocks, Christine. 2010. *Interviews in qualitative research.* London: Sage.

Kovach, Margaret E. 2009. *Indigenous methodologies: Characteristics, conversations, and contexts.* Toronto: University of Toronto Press.

Kusow, Abdi. 2003. Beyond indigenous authenticity: Reflections on the insider/outsider debate in immigration research. *Symbolic Interaction 26*, 4: 591–599.

Miczo, Nathan. 2003. Beyond the "fetishism of words": Considerations on the use of the interview to gather chronic illness narratives. *Qualitative Health Research 13*, 4: 469–490.

Morse, Janice M., and Penrod, Janice. 1999. Linking concepts of enduring, uncertainty, suffering, and hope. *Image: The Journal of Nursing Scholarship 31*, 2: 145–150.

Olson, Karin. 2011. *Essentials of qualitative interviewing.* Walnut Creek, CA: Left Coast Press.

Potter, Jonathan, and Hepburn, Alexa. 2012. Eight challenges for interview researchers. In *Handbook of Interview Research 2nd ed.* (pp. 555–570), Jaber F. Gubrium, James A. Holstein, Amir B. Marvasti, and Karyn D. Marvasti eds. Thousand Oaks, CA: Sage.

Priya, Kumar R. 2010. The research relationship as a facilitator of remoralization and self-growth: Postearthquake suffering and healing. *Qualitative Health Research 20*, 4: 479–495.

Saldaña, Johnny. 2014. Blue-collar qualitative research: A rant. *Qualitative Inquiry 20*, 8: 976–980.

Seidman, Irving E. 2015. *Interviewing as qualitative research 4th ed.* New York: Teachers College Press.

Sered, Susan. 2014. Suffering in an age of personal responsibility. *Contexts 14*, 2: 37–43.

Smith, Linda T. 2005. On tricky ground: Researching the native in the age of uncertainty. In *Handbook of Qualitative Research 3rd ed.* (pp. 85–107), Norman K. Denzin and Yvonna Lincoln eds. Thousand Oaks, CA: Sage.

Smith, Linda T. 1999. *Decolonizing methodologies: Research and indigenous peoples.* London: Zed Books.

Snow, David, and Moss, Dana. 2014. Protest on the fly: Toward a theory of spontaneity in the dynamics of protest and social movements. *American Sociological Review 79*, 6: 1122–1143.

St. Pierre, Elizabeth A., and Jackson, Alecia Y. 2014. Qualitative data analysis after coding. *Qualitative Inquiry 20*, 6: 715–719.

Wasserman, Jason A., and Clair, Jeffrey M. 2013. The insufficiency of fairness: The logics of homeless service administration and resulting gaps in service. *Culture and Organization 19*, 2: 179–180.

Wasserman, Jason A., and Clair, Jeffrey M. 2010. *At home on the street: People, poverty, and a hidden culture of homelessness.* Boulder, CO: Lynne Rienner Publishers.

Weber, Max. 1968. *Economy and society*, Guenther Roth and Claus Wittich eds. Berkeley: University of California Press.

Weldes, Jutta. 1989. Marxism and methodological individualism: A critique. *Theory and Society 18*, 3: 353–386.

Williams, Gareth. 2006. Suffering sociologists and the sociology of suffering. *Medical Sociology Online 1*, 1: 39–41. www.medicalsociologyonline.org/oldsite/archives/issue11/suffsoc.html.

SECTION II

Methodological Interventions

4

POETIC INQUIRY

Transforming Qualitative Data Into Poetry

Valerie J. Janesick

Introduction

Qualitative researchers are expanding the repertoire of techniques used in data representation, analysis, and interpretation as we capture the lived experience of our participants. Poetry is one way to capture social inquiry. For example, the use of **found data poems (FDP)**—that is, poetry found in the narrative, spoken, or visual text—may transform data from the researcher's reflective journal, the interview transcripts, and any site documents used in a given study. Found poetry offers another way of viewing and presenting data. In addition, **identity poetry, also called I Poetry**, may likewise add to our repertoire of techniques in capturing our own stories as researchers in a given study. Furthermore, participants in a study may create some identity poetry to offer yet another data set for analysis and interpretation. Qualitative researchers are now finding ways to use and design poetic inquiry (see Bishop & Willis, 2014; Glesne, 1997; Nicol, 2008; Prendergast, 2006). In this chapter, I write about ways to understand, conceptualize, explore, and expand our notions of poetic ways of seeing and knowing. While I will concentrate mostly on found poetry and identity poetry, other styles of poetry may be discussed. We will begin with dialogue and reflection on poetry to magnify lived experience.

Why Use Poetry in Research?

Since Aristotle argued that poetry is truer than history, writers have been using poetry to depict life as we experience it. For me as a qualitative researcher, I have been thinking about ways to use interview transcripts and other written or spoken words in new ways. Because poetry may capture the miraculous, the surprising, and the essence of everyday life, why not use poetry to represent that interview data, data from the researcher's journal, and other texts such as emails, Facebook posts, and so forth?

Poetry uses the words of everyday life and goes further with these words in terms of using metaphor, possibly rhyme, and various rigorous structures to call our attention to the meaning of life. Poetry is a way to find out what a person means to say as well as what a person means when he or she speaks the words. The rhythm, the beat, and the sound of poetry awaken us to the beautiful in life and make us tap into our imaginations. If we look at the transcript of an interview, for example, the participant in a given study gives us a good deal of data. Why not take the words of the transcript and transform those words into a found data poem? In addition, some researchers (Furman, 2006, 2007; Furman et al., 2007; Furman, Lietz, & Langer, 2006; Maynard & Cahnmann-Taylor, 2010; Young, D. 2010) are calling poetry itself a form of inquiry. Furthermore, social scientists, such as Bochner (2002), call this approach poetic social science. He points out that basically by using poetry or any alternative to traditional approaches to research, we add to our knowledge of the social world. Likewise, as Eisner (2004) mentions, the ways we represent things eventually have an effect on how we perceive them and, of course, how we make meaning:

> There is no single legitimate way to make sense of the world. Different ways of seeing give us different worlds. Different ways of saying, allow us to represent different worlds. A novel as well as a statistical mean can enlarge human understanding.
>
> *(p. 5)*

Another reason to attach oneself to poetry is that it is an ancient technique with a long and dependable history indicating its importance for the humanity of each individual on earth, for as T.S. Elliot (1920) once wrote: "Genuine poetry can communicate before it is understood."

But first, why should we even be talking about poetry in research to begin with? One might ask, Why are we doing this again? Perhaps the character of John Keating, played by Robin Williams in the Hollywood film (1989) *Dead Poet's Society*, said it forcefully: "We don't read and write poetry because it's cute. We read and write poetry because we are members of the human race. And the human race is filled with passion." In the film, set in a Northeastern United States academy, Keating inspires his students to appreciate and love poetry and to write and read poetry. He advises that the reason to write poetry is to *make their lives extraordinary*. I venture to say that in the future we should make room for poetry in our qualitative researcher courses and our research projects. We as qualitative researchers are engaged in passionate work in that we are attempting to capture the lived experience of another human being in a given social context. In that process of capturing life through poetry, we can count on a few things.

1. **Poetry is about life and allows for building relationships and community**. By the very act of writing and reading aloud a piece of poetry in a group such as a classroom, a duet made of researcher and participant, or any group public venue, we are on the road to making a relationship and ultimately building a community of poets. Poetry was never meant to be published in a tiny book and left on a shelf. Poetry is meant to be part of life, and, in this case, it could easily be part of any qualitative research narrative. Furthermore it recalls Keating's idea that we can make life extraordinary through the writing and performance of poetry. By that very act, we engage an audience, a community if you will. We also may make our work more understandable to some by way of using poetry.

2. **Poetry brings beauty into our everyday lives**. How can it not do so? To read, write, and hear poetry, we already move into the artistic mode. We use words in new ways and take the ordinary stuff of daily life and make it extraordinary. In a world transfixed with digital gadgets, games, and distractions, poetry offers an alternative. That alternative allows us to recognize the beautiful in daily living. In order to recognize the beautiful, it is important to slow down, calm down, and find a space to write your poetry based on the data in your study.

3. **Poetry opens up ways to see the world and makes a space for the spoken word as well as the written word.** You as a poet will read aloud your poetry, and that very act opens up a new look at social reality. It also means you are engaged actively in making meaning of something in the social world. Rather than sitting on a sofa and watching television, playing video games, or becoming a bystander in life, the poet is engaged in life and is anxious to represent it poetically. Poetry allows us to forget about being a bystander in life and to actually take part in life. To use one example of the power of the spoken word of written poetry, take a look at the open mic (open microphone) evenings at your local coffeehouse or on the World Wide Web 2.0. Communities are seeing the value of having the spoken word as part of any evening that features local talent.[1]

4. **Poetry as inquiry builds resilience and sparks imagination and creativity**. Poetry is imaginative and forces you the writer to be creative and push your imagination somewhere it has never been before. Creativity is active. It includes successes and failures. I am reminded of the classic story about Thomas Edison who tested over 10,000 substances to create a light bulb that would not explode. Fellow scientists asked him how he could fail so many times. His reply captures this perfectly. He said that in fact he did not fail at all. He merely discovered 10,000 things that simply did not work. I think of creativity as a habit and have written of this elsewhere (Janesick, 2016). Most often creativity can be viewed in three ways: First, creativity may be approached in ordinary conversation or writing by individuals with a curious mind. Second, personal creativity is that form of creativity an

individual may experience by experiencing the world and life in original and novel ways without writing about it or speaking of it. Third, creativity may be viewed as referring to those individuals who change our world by inventions or written texts like noteworthy artists or scientists. Think of Steve Jobs, Pablo Picasso, or Diana Gabaldon, for example. The creative habit, and the creative act such as writing poetry, must be exercised and sharpened and a willingness to fail thought of as a type of creativity. What is amazing about creativity is that it takes so many forms and formats. No one researcher, no one writer, no one poet makes quite the same statement. Thus, there is a generative quality to poetry that widens our knowledge base and our understanding of our worlds.

5. **Poetry leads to awareness and self-knowledge, which leads to social justice awareness with effort on the poet's part at least.** One of the amazing things about teaching qualitative research methods throughout my career is the realization that each research project, each dissertation committee I serve on, and any workshop I conduct leads closer to self-knowledge and the ability to articulate that knowledge. This becomes useful when describing the role of the researcher. Every one of our projects needs to have a segment where the research clearly describes the role of the researcher in the research project. Poetry can very easily assist in that process and not just with writing an identity poem. Any section of a project can be enhanced by the use of poetry. Likewise, by going deeper into an understanding of the self, a poet/researcher may come a bit closer to understanding social justice and advocating for social justice. Many poets have in fact been agents of change through poetry. Not to name everyone, but consider poets such as Walt Whitman, Sylvia Plath, E.E. Cummings, Keats, Aristophanes, and Shakespeare. These are people who uncovered inequality in their own time frame, and the meaning lasts beyond their years on this earth. Social justice themes are seen in much of the poetry for open mic competitions.[2]

In this respect, it becomes clearer as to how poetry might be integrated into our qualitative research projects. Specifically, two types of poetry are user friendly and may encourage the most reluctant researcher to see data from interview transcripts, observations, photographs, the spoken word, or site documents in a new way. First let us review found data poetry.

What Is Found Data Poetry?

Found data poetry is poetry found in interview transcripts, in documents from the research site, in performances, and in any spoken or visual text relevant to the research project. For example, someone's resume or curriculum vitae, their emails, policy documents, and participants' written statements and reflective journals may be fodder for a found data poem (see Janesick, 2016). Many in the field of arts-based research (ABR) have led the way in describing and validating poetry as a form of inquiry. Of all the art forms, poetry is quite suited to representing the mind and ideas. Poetry engages us and draws us into someone's life experience. With any given set of words, the poet rearranges those words and develops a found poem. In this example, I wrote this poem following two workshops and at least two dozen classes with a favorite yoga teacher. I took notes at the workshops, during classes, and after classes. It is part of a series on finding poetry in various texts. I call this poem "Yoga Rules." A version of this poem appeared in my book, *Contemplative Qualitative Inquiry: Practicing the Zen of Research* (2015).

Yoga Rules

Locate your spine, says the teacher,
Energetically push your kidneys into the mat.
Lean into the prominent information of your body.

Educate your 2nd toe,
Hang around in that pose for sometime.

Notice your disorganized thinking
Activate the interior of your floating ribs.
Let your thigh muscles scream.

Let your heart hang humbly forward.
Listen to the limits of your body.
Now stimulate the bone tissue in your left leg.

Use the entire periphery of your skin
As you roll from side to side.
Visualize the axis of your spine.

Use your skin to bring data to your self.
Address your right hip
And investigate your breath.

Step into your emotions
And keep your brain cool.
Make your sit bones really hear.

Permit your body to do its natural thing,
Stay for some time in the bones.
Your breath is like a horse and
Your mind is its rider.
When it wanders, rein it in.

Feel your connective tissues
Under the muscles
And make your energy unpolluted.

Breath into the edges of your diaphragm
Make your body more radiant,
Locate and educate your spine.

Another type of found poetry can be created directly from an interview transcript; in the example that follows, it is found in an interview transcript from the oral history interview of a New York first responder after the 9/11 attacks.[3] The *New York Times* has available, to anyone, over 500 transcripts for understanding the perspectives of the first responders. It is an open-access site fought over for five years. The first responders triumphed in the court battle to make these transcripts available for all. I use these examples in my classes to illustrate how to create poetry from interview transcripts and/or documents. See this example from a first responder nurse followed by poems found in the data.

Example: Excerpt from a Transcript of an Interview with EMT, Diane DeMarco, Nurse. Interview Date, December 14, 2001.

Q: Diane, can you tell me what happened that day?

A: . . . When I arrived at the outpost, there was a call given of, I think it's a 1040, plane into building. Shortly after that I was assigned to the job. . . . I was working with another EMT, Thomas Lopez. . . . We had gotten to the location of Vesey and West. There was really no one in charge down there. We were basically in charge of ourselves, which worked out pretty well. A supervisor had been passing us by . . . he directed us into the building, the second floor of the building with our equipment.

I don't know what happened. A couple of minutes after that, I saw my partner get his bags and start towards the building. I told him—I had turned around myself. I had started to go get my tech bag, and I realized this is not a good idea. . . . Shortly—I don't know, it would have been minutes, seconds after we turned the vehicle around, the first building fell, the first collapse. At that point there was a car blocking the area, and I was going to attempt to turn that vehicle around. It belonged to a chief that had just passed me by. I knew that he was in front of the hotel. . . . I attempted to walk toward the hotel, but just as I attempted to do that the—I don't know what to call it, the mushroom, avalanche thing was coming at us. I turned around and called to my partner. We got back in the vehicle and started to pull away from the scene. . . . I noticed several Fire Department personnel, firemen, walking aimlessly or sitting on the corner of where I had pulled in. I don't know the location . . . so I started to take firemen off the street corners wherever I was finding them. They were totally covered in dust, caked, on their eyelids. So my partner and I again started to treat people . . . as we were doing that the second tower collapsed. So everybody scattered, and they started running . . . and we got into the vehicle and started to drive off. . . . I think that's where I got to Chambers Street, after the second collapse.

★★★ End of excerpt.

When you think about our work as qualitative researchers, one of the surprises in any given interview is what you might find. In this example, a nurse goes to work like any other day, but what happens that day affects her for life. Again, the immediacy of the description offers food for poetry. From the excerpt above, see this example of a found poem I was inspired to write.

An Ordinary Blue Sky

An ordinary blue sky
Two buildings collapse
Everything changes.

To summarize this section and move on, found data poems are poems found in transcripts, notes, researcher reflective journals, observations, and any site documents such as emails, curriculum vitae, course syllabi, social media postings, or photographs. Let us now turn to another valuable tool in the poet's toolkit, the identity poem.

What Is Identity Poetry?

Identity poetry, sometimes known as I Poetry, is gaining ground in the arts, sciences, and education. Identity poetry is a good fit for the qualitative researcher since it may be used in many places in a narrative report. For example, identity poetry may be used by participants to describe their role in the project or to reflect their ideas given prompts by the researcher. It may capture entire stories of participants' lives. It may be used by the researcher as well when describing the researcher's role or to illustrate a key finding.

See this example of a prompt for getting an individual to write an identity poem. The first step is to start. Then take baby steps till you write your first poem!

Example: Identity Poetry Activity

Where I am from

I am from (ordinary item) _____

I am from (home adjective) _____

I am from (plant, flower) _____
I am from (family tradition) _____
I am from the (family tendency) _____
I am from (something you were told as a child) _____
I am from (spiritual tradition) _____
I am from (ethnicity) _____
I am from (place of birth) _____
I am from (two food items representing your family) _____

_____
I am from stories about _____
I am from (memories you have) _____.

I have used this for workshops, for presentations, and in classes and ask for volunteers to read their poems. This is like a warm-up exercise for getting them accustomed to writing anything that resembles a poem. Many find that reading the poem is astonishingly powerful. Identity poetry is a valuable strategy and tool for capturing the lived experience of participants and researchers alike. In fact for me, both found data poems and identity poems are about beginnings and endings. In found poetry, a poem may signify the lived experience of a participant through its beginnings, its endings, and what is omitted. Poetry is often about what is left out of any final report or narrative. A poetic writer may find the use of poetry one of the best ways to get the reader involved in reading the research at hand. A poet in the end immerses the reader of the poem into the actual experience of everyday living.

Example: Identity Poetry in Spanish and English

See this example written by Elizabeth Visedo (2015) about her origin in Janesick (2016). Elizabeth was born and grew up in Argentina. She has traveled the world and lived on at least three continents. She completed her doctorate at the University of South Florida studying bi-literacy.

Origen

Soy de tardes de mate amargo y bizcochitos
de la tierra del tango y el malbec
Soy de jazmín y berro
y a baldear la vereda y a regar
Pinoluz e incienso
de zarzuelas, Piazzola y Spinetta
Soy de parroquia, del estado y del mundo
del oeste, la quinta y la pileta
Soy del sur, la injusticia y el sueño
de ganar en la Davis y de River campeón

Soy de revolución y utopías
de Pichuco, Serrat y Simone de Beauvoir
de invierno confesiones y una noche en la opera
De tiros, gritos y golpes y mordazas
Soy de los pecados mortales y secretos
del incesto, el abuso y el suicidio
Soy de una dictadura militar de siete años
con miles de meses sin carnaval
Soy de la chacarera y el Río de la Plata
la locura, el inglés y el desarraigo
las palizas de mama y las caricias de Mome
secándome las lágrimas sin retorno.

Origin

I am from the afternoons
of unsweetened "mate" tea and lard biscuits
From the land of tango and Malbec
I'm from jasmines and watercress
to wash the sidewalk and water the plants
Pinesol and incense
from operettas, Piazzola and Spinetta
I'm from the Rosary parish, the state, the world
from the West country-houses with pool
I'm from the South, injustice, and the dream
to win the Davis Cup with River as champion
I am from revolution and utopias
from Pichuco, Serrat, Simone de Beauvoir
from Winter Confessions and A Night at the Opera
from gunshots, screams, coups, blows and muzzles
I am from deadly sins and secrets
from incest, abuse and suicide
I'm from a seven years long dictatorship
with thousands of months with no Carnival
I'm from "chacarera" and Río de la Plata
madness, English and rootlessness
my mom's spanking and the neighbor's caress
wiping out my tears with no way back.

This example of identity poetry illustrates how a researcher might use poetry to describe self-awareness and her or his role in the research project.

Identity poetry may be useful for qualitative researchers if for no other reason than to describe their own role in a research project. Furthermore, participants may also find that writing a poem to describe themselves may assist in recalling pertinent issues and meaning for the project at hand. See this powerful example of Rachel Rostad's identity poem "Names" (https://www.youtube.com/watch?v=gfexOa8-h44). It would be difficult to miss the beat, the meaning, and the strength of this identity poem.

Or see this poem, "Fat Girl" (https://www.youtube.com/watch?v=vxgpCf PqQpk). As an example of an identity poem, Megan Falley identifies for us her interpretation of a life as a fat girl. The point I am trying to make here is that identity poetry can be an eye opener and a mind opener for individuals who wish to go a bit further in identifying their own stories.

Identity Poetry as Dialogic Poetry

Another form of identity poem for consideration is that of dialogic poetry. Ward (2014) conducted a life history project in which the main participant was a visual artist, poet, and teacher. He studied how she influenced educational leaders and her legacy. He asked her to write a poem, and he would respond, and so on and on, back and forth with each other. Here is a segment of a lengthy poem of hers about what might be her legacy and then his response, also a segment of a longer poem. He calls his participant Nina.

Example of Dialogic Identity Poetry

Nina's first poem:

On Building Dovetailed Corners with August Wilson

Dove-tailed corners
A father's advice on well-built furniture is good to remember—
(Heed)
"It's those little details that only God notices"
hidden misericords on medieval benches
resting perch for tired ecclesiastics
mid-tierce or matins amens
a high hallelujah of Latin and you hold that syllable a bit too long
a yawn in God's house
gargoyles only the dove sees cooing high above the city
one shiny patterned slice of architectural folderol
a buttonhole perfectly stitched with ruby twist
(hidden under the flamboyant Czech bohemian glass button)
Ah, August Wilson knows the perfectly finished dovecote
Or the plowed field that from above is a plumb line to God
My grandmother won't let me shortchange the art—
(perhaps that hem that is just uneven turned up material)
Blasphemy

It honors neither the fabric nor the craft
And that is the key—
Pithy intention
He cried that keening moan of knowing
"limitation of the instrument"
It's the dance of creator and creation—

Ward's response:

On Cutting (Dovetailed) Corners

They sit there . . . unnoticed,
with matching grain,
sanded and smooth—
tight-fitted joints: the interlocking of
Artistry and Craft.
Folded in on one another as if they are
inseparable hands of prayer.

But the dovetailed corners of teaching—
The bob and the weave;
The zig and the zag;
The warp and the woof
have been cut (we cut corners, you know?)

Replaced by a craftless metric
that is the new ruler.
And the plumbed depths sound no twain,
shallow pools reflecting the pedantic apothecary
from whence they've come—
    that prescribes
    and demarcates
how new corners are made.

They are still here . . . interlocked
But
looser—with a certain roughness
that comes from dotting I's and crossing T's . . .

Here you have seen a fine example of the use of dialogic poetry to capture the main participant's identity and her meaning followed by the response of the researcher that captures his understanding of a portion of that legacy. There is no limit to the possibilities of the use of identity poetry in qualitative research projects.

Future Possibilities for Poetry and the Qualitative Researcher

Just looking at these two types of poetry, found data poetry and identity poetry, you can imagine the potential for the qualitative researcher—not just the option of using poetry in interpreting data or capturing cases, for example, but also using poetry to capture the role of the researchers and participants. Should we stop there? I think not. Why not use poetry to frame and capture the literature review? Why not use poetry to capture the description of the method of a study? See this example of haiku: 17-syllable Japanese poems on method. De Felice (2012) studied endangered languages in Mexico and implications for educators. Throughout the study, he wrote poetry to track his reflections on method. Here are five of his haiku.

My Study

My super study
Surprises, strengths, savvy and
Serendipitous.

On Translations

English-Espanol
Hmmm, Que hago-which to use
I hardly know when.

On Terminology

My participants
Culture and language experts
Nahuatlor Mayan.

On Transcribing

Dragon voice two laps
English-Espanol my voice
Their words, their languages.

On Text Analysis

Text analysis,
Cyclical and immersive,
Looking for essence.

Overall, you can see here potential for the use of poetry throughout the research process.

Continuing on with my questions, I ask, why not use poetry to introduce and/or conclude cases developed from qualitative data? Of course there are many example of researchers (Prendergast, 2006; Furman, 2006) already started on that path. I hope you are ready and willing to try poetry in qualitative research at various points that make sense. In the future I would like to write further about the use of haiku and all other forms of Japanese poetry. But until then, find a quiet place, sit down, and meditate for a few minutes—look over your data and start a poem.

Notes

1 To see a powerful example of the speaking of poetry in this vein, see Rachel Finley at an open mic competition, such as the one seen here—https://www.youtube.com/watch?v=_Nu45Dume5s.
2 See, for example, Rachel Rostad's poem to J.K. Rowling: https://www.youtube.com/watch?v=iFPWwx96Kew.
3 The site that holds all the stories of the first responders can be found at http://graphics8.nytimes.com/packages/html/nyregion/20050812_WTC_GRAPHIC/met_WTC_histories_full_01.html.

References

Bishop, E. C. & Willis, K. F. (2014). "Hope is that fiery feeling:" Using poetry as data to explore the meanings of hope for young people. *Forum: Qualitative Social Research,* *15*(1), Art. 9. Retrieved from http://www.qualitative-research.net/index.php/fqs/article/view/2013/3631.

Bochner, A. (2002). Criteria against ourselves. *Qualitative Inquiry.* Vol. 6, pp. 278–291.

De Felice, D. (2012). *A phenomenological study of teaching endangered languages online: Perspectives from Nahua and Mayan educators.* (Doctoral dissertation). Retrieved from http://scolarcommns.usf.edu/etd/4465/.

Eisner, E.W. (2004) *The arts and creation of mind.* New Haven: Yale University Press.

Eliot, T. S. (1920[2009]). *The sacred wood: Essays on poetry and criticism.* New York: Dodo Press.

Furman, R. (2006). Poetic forms and structures in qualitative health research. *Qualitative Health Research.* Vol. 16, No. 4, pp. 560–566.

Furman, R. (2007). Poetry and narrative as qualitative data: Exploration into existential theory. *The Indo-Pacific Journal of Phenomenology.* Vol. 7, No. 1, pp. 1–9.

Furman, R., Langer, C. L., Davis, C. S., Gallardo, H. P., & Shanti, K. (2007). Expressive, research and reflective poetry as qualitative inquiry: A study of adolescent identity. *Qualitative Research.* Vol. 7, No. 3, pp. 301–315.

Furman, R., Lietz, C., & Langer, C. (2006). The research poem in international social work: Innovations in qualitative methodology. *International Journal of Qualitative Methods.* Vol. 5, No. 3, Article 3.

Glesne, C. (1997). That rare feeling: Re-presenting research through poetic transcription. *Qualitative Inquiry.* Vol. 3, No. 2, pp. 202–221.

Janesick, V. J. (2015). *Contemplative qualitative inquiry: Practicing the Zen of research*. Walnut Creek, CA: Left Coast Press.

Janesick, V. J. (2016). *Stretching exercises for qualitative researchers, 4th ed.* Thousand Oaks, CA: Sage.

Maynard, K., & Cahnmann-Taylor, M. (2010). Anthropology at the edge of words: Where poetry and ethnography meet. *Anthropology Humanism*. Vol. 35, No. 1, pp. 2–19.

Nicol, J. J. (2008). Creating vocative texts. *The Qualitative Report*. Vol. 13, No. 3, pp. 316–333.

Prendergast, M. (2006). Found poetry as literature review: Research poems on audience and performance. *Qualitative Inquiry*. Vol. 12, No. 2, pp. 369–388.

Ward, D. (2014). *Teaching with the end in mind: A teacher's life history as a legacy of educational leaders*. (Unpublished doctoral dissertation). University of South Florida, Tampa.

Young, D. (2010). *The art of recklessness: Poetry as assertive force and contradiction*. Minneapolis, MN: Graywolf Press.

5

EMERGENT LISTENING

Bronwyn Davies

In this chapter, I explore the epistemology and ontology of selves *emergent in the space of listening*, of what I call *emergent listening*, through which the not-yet-known might open up. Such listening involves a radical break from who you are as listener and from usual ways of making sense of difference. Not all modes of 'listening' afford the listener and the listened-to the emergent possibilities I am exploring here. Listening-as-usual is listening that presumes it knows already what anyone might say or mean; it is actively engaged in the formation of selves within already known categories. It is the listening that has become dominant in our contemporary age of neoliberal capitalism (Davies & Gannon, 2009). These more familiar modes of listening hold things the same and, intentionally or otherwise, uphold the normative order.

Although it is emergent listening I want to explore here, I am not mounting an either/or argument or proposing a hierarchy between them. I will suggest that both modes of listening are necessary, and even depend on one another, even while at least partially undoing each other. The repetition of the same and the emergence of the new are contrary yet interdependent lines of force. When one takes over as the only mode of listening, however, there is a problem. I will come back to this thought when I introduce Bergson's (1998) lines of *ascent* and *descent*.

In thinking my way through the concept and practice of emergent listening, I am inspired by Jean-Luc Nancy (2007) to think of emergent listening as listening with *all* one's senses—as a multi-sensual encounter with the world, and not as a self separate from the world but as a self emergent with/in the world, open to the world: "To be listening is to be at the same time outside and inside, to be open from without and from within, hence from one to the other and from one in the other" (Nancy, 2007, p. 14). And inspired by Deleuze (1994), I see the self as "a threshold, a door, a becoming between two" (Deleuze & Guattari, 1987, p. 249).

A final conceptual key to emergent listening comes with the taking up of Barad's move from reflexivity to diffraction.

Deleuze and Difference

In my exploration of emergent listening, I want to place *difference* at the heart of things. To accomplish this conceptual shift, I draw on Deleuze, who urged a move away from difference understood as categorical difference, toward difference as continuous movement, as ongoing *differenciation*, in which we both singularly and as multiplicities go on becoming different. In *Difference and Repetition* (1994), Deleuze had argued that difference has long been seen as a secondary characteristic, which only emerges when one compares pre-existing things. This network of comparisons between pre-conceived categorical identities obscures a much more subtle and involuted network of *emergent* differences that are opened up in acts of what I want to map out here as emergent listening.

Emergent listening is slow, ethical listening; it requires of us to dwell in the moment of the pause before difference emerges. To explore this moment, Deleuze invoked the concept of *haecceity*—the moment when the difference between this and that, body and horizon, shifts. Dwelling in that space of openness to difference, in the space in between one and another, was integral to his conception of ethics. Ethics is not a matter of prescribed behavior based on always remaining the same within prescribed limits, and within the already-formed/already-known, but an affective openness to the other in which one asks, simply, "What is it to be this?"

Barad and Diffraction

Barad, a physicist and philosopher, gives us the concept of *diffraction*. Diffraction also invites a radical conceptual shift from usual ways of thinking about life—no longer an endless set of repetitions with minor variations, but *movement itself*. Barad (2003) cites Haraway: "Diffraction does not produce 'the same' displaced, as reflection and refraction do. Diffraction is a mapping of interference, not of replication, reflection, or reproduction" (1992, p. 300). In this sense, diffractive practice and thought opens the self to *interference* or becoming different to what one was before.

Barad thus invites us to go beyond reflection, or reflexivity, which is implicitly based on the phenomenon of a pattern of light that reflects an actual, pre/existing object or entity. The task of reflexive researchers is to *represent* what is already there, in objects or individuals, including the researcher. Representation acts as a conservative force, since it works with categorically defined/de-limited entities. On the basis of physics experiments with light, Barad observes, "Reflection is insufficient; intervention is the key" (2007, p. 50). Diffraction, in contrast to reflection or reflexivity, does not reproduce an image of what is imagined to be already there but is focused on its ongoing production. So Barad takes us further in the direction Deleuze sets out, toward thinking of movement as primary, and to a focus on the moment when the new emerges. Diffraction is, moreover, intractably entangled and intra-active.

We are so used to using reflection and reflexivity as the primary conceptual and practical analytic tools of qualitative research, that shifting to diffraction as metaphor and practice makes for a significant interference in thinking-as-usual—and listening-as-usual. Whereas reflection and reflexivity might document *difference*— that is, difference between things located in already established categories— diffraction involves itself in the process whereby a *difference is made*. It is therefore a study not of completed subjects or objects but of subjects or objects in the making. This is a conceptual shift, which "unsettles the metaphysics of individualism," by claiming that individuals "do not pre-exist as such but rather materialise in intra-action" (Barad, 2012a, p. 77). A diffractive approach, Barad argues, opens an onto-epistemological space of *encounter*.

The concept of *encounter* is significant here, focusing attention on the ongoing intra-active processes through which selves come into being and go on coming into being in complex emergent relationality. The diffractive researcher's task is not to tell of something that exists independent of the research encounter but to access that which is becoming true, ontologically *and* epistemologically, in the moment of the encounter. A research encounter in this sense is experimental— the researcher does not know in advance what onto-epistemological knowledge will emerge from it. And as such it involves us in emergent listening:

> So while it is true that diffraction apparatuses [of physics] measure the effects of difference, even more profoundly they highlight, exhibit, and make evident the entangled structure of the changing and contingent ontology of the world, including the ontology of knowing. In fact, diffraction not only brings the reality of entanglements to light, it is itself an entangled phenomenon.
>
> *(Barad, 2007, p. 73)*

As researchers and practitioners listening to difference as it emerges, we are, in Barad's terms, becoming part of "the entangled structure of the changing and contingent ontology of the world, including the ontology of knowing" (2007, p. 73). To listen in an emergent way is to be open to that entanglement, that changing and contingent ontology, and the changing and contingent ways of knowing and being that encounters can open us up to.

Barad's concepts, along with Deleuzian concepts, offer tools for opening up a way of thinking and being in which discourses, practices, and ethics—like particles of light, ripples on a pond, or criss-crossing waves on the ocean—affect each other: they *interfere* with each other. Ideas and matter affect each other. And just as ripples and waves and drops of foam do not exist without the body of water, or the wind, or the other matter they encounter (stones, sand, rocks, human bodies . . .), we, as social science researchers and practitioners, are part of, and encounter, already entangled matter and meanings that affect us, and that we affect, in an ongoing, always changing set of movements: "Mattering is simultaneously a matter of substance and significance" (Barad, 2007, p. 3).

A diffractive analysis seeks to locate the lines of force that are at play, along with their effects on each other. It draws attention to the lines of force through which we are each, singly and as entangled multiplicities, produced through these encounters, always in process of becoming-other-than-we-were-before. Each movement across a threshold, between one and another, potentially contributes to the creative evolutionary force of each one and of the creative evolutionary force of the community as a whole. Looked at in this way, the world is in continuous motion, changing in multiple intersecting encounters. Yet the social order *also* has a remarkable capacity to stay the same, which brings me full circle back to my opening remarks about "listening-as-usual."

Bergson and Lines of Descent and Ascent

To understand the way emergent differences and changes can be continually folded back into the existing social order, Bergson (1998) gave us the concepts of lines of force, and in particular lines of *descent* and *ascent*. Lines of descent are made up out of more or less automatic repetitions, while lines of ascent take off into the not-yet-known. He emphasizes, on the one hand, the *necessary interdependence* of these two lines of force. On the other, he argues that *the creative evolution of life, of thought and of being*, emerges not from docile conformity to pre-conceived norms, the line of descent, but from the surprising and new, the line of ascent. Regularity and repetition, the lines of descent, create the familiar liveable world by holding things the same. Creative lines of flight that open up new modes of thought and ways of being, the lines of ascent, give life its energy, its creative life-force. The lines of ascent are, at one and the same time, necessary for life, sometimes dangerous, and always subject to being re-territorialized and thus re-incorporated back into lines of descent, to habitual repetitions. It's a constant entangled movement—rarely either/or.

Deleuze and Guattari (1987) extend Bergson's thinking about lines of ascent and descent with their concepts of de- and re-territorialization. If we listen to children at play and at work, it is difficult not to see the endless repetitions through which they become skilled at taking up their allocated position within the social order. Those repetitive practices shape the normative embodied subjects anticipated by, and required within, the social *order*. The normative, binary modes of speech and thought that the social order, and listening-as-usual, depend on normalize and naturalize any number of binaries and the hierarchical positioning of individuals within them—the gender binary, for example, and the "abled" / "disabled" binary—as if we were all, somehow, naturally and from the beginning one or the other.

The territorialization of individualized selves make the normative world appear both natural and morally superior. It seems natural, and desirable, when girls are "feminine" and play games that invent and reiterate material and relational order in shops and kitchens, or when boys are "masculine" and play team games developing the intimate knowledge of risk-taking and tribal warfare. To accomplish and maintain the social order, as we know it, each subject, singly and in intra-action with others, practices modes of enunciation and bodily practices through which the perfectly honed subject becomes recognizable within the gendered and other normative lines of force that run through the collective body.

Creative evolution, however, Bergson argues, rests on a capacity to let go of the repetitive, stratified status quo. That letting go creates a deep opening for new possibilities when fixed identities and fixed patterns no longer hold everything the same: where what one understands by oneself and the other are vibrant, emergent materialities engaged in mattering (Bennett, 2010). In that mobility, in that intra-active becoming, the ethical questioning of what is being made to matter in any encounter is an ongoing ethical responsibility.

Listening to Children at Play: The Gendered Play of Difference

Selves are called to order within the collective body, and the body of each self is progressively territorialized—made to make sense within existing modes of enunciation, made into a subject in effect. The potency of the lines of force through which order is created cannot be underestimated. The ontological-epistemological accomplishment of self as belonging in whatever categories one has been assigned becomes real very quickly. Listening to children at play, listening with all our senses, we encounter one of the most recognizable features, which is the ongoing rehearsal of the skills necessary to ensure recognition of themselves within those categories they have been assigned, enabling them to live out the identification of self within any number of binary stratifications, endlessly rehearsing the specificity of their positioning within the existing repetitive order. This play/work that they do, territorializing their bodies and their thoughts and emotions, is necessary work; and it also binds them into categories that in part run counter to what Bergson calls creative evolution. They are the stabilizing line of descent; but they also need the lines of ascent to keep them alive, to open up moments of creative evolution, indeed to make capitalism work. The line of ascent is also necessary for any kind of social change—for changes that might enable us to go beyond current inequities that are the lot of non-normatively embodied subjects—those whose identities are defined as subordinate in any number of social binaries, and those whose identities lie outside the epistemologies and ontologies of identity-making within the normative social order.

It is important to grasp in this dynamic relation between lines of ascent and descent that the territorializing lines of force or lines of descent are not only, or even primarily, experienced as oppressive. Rather, they are very often "comforting: they enable the chaos of the world to be reduced to discrete categories of meaning and structure. They are also necessary, for they enable us to interact with the social world; to form relations with others and to have a political 'voice'" (Malins, 2007, p. 153). *At the same time* they "reduce the range of connections a body can make with the world around it; diminishing its potential for difference and becoming-other" (Malins, 2007, p. 153). And for some that diminishing is utterly oppressive. We all need both lines of force, that which is repetitive and that which risks the new. As I said at the outset, in this current neoliberal moment, there is an enormous press toward the former, toward becoming generic individualized competitive subjects within neoliberal regimes—recognizable through our conformity to endless regulations and measurements that shape us up as always-yet-more-productive.

What we usually think of as listening—that is, listening-as-usual, particularly as adults listening to children—is most closely aligned with lines of descent; we listen in order to fit what we hear into what we already know and to judge it accordingly. Listening that opens up lines of ascent, or that de-territorializes normative assumptions and practices, is what I am calling emergent listening. This involves working, to some extent, against oneself and against those habitual practices through which one establishes 'this is who I am' and 'this is who you are.'

De-territorializing or ascending lines of force, which open up the possibility of transformation or creative evolution, cannot be specified in advance. Transformations are usually of a molecular kind, not putting an end to repetitive and static lines of descent, but finding the movement possible within and against them. The gender assemblage, like any other assemblage, depends on molecular shifts to keep it alive and in motion. Stratified systems, no matter how rigid they seem, need movement. Children's play and learning not only is repetitive but also holds potential for difference and becoming-other—for differenciation.

The episode of children's play that I will explore here comes from *Trollet*—a Reggio Emilia inspired preschool in the south east of Sweden (Davies, 2014). The central protagonist is Francesca, who at first appears totally taken over by the categorization of girl. Her hair, her dress, and her personal style appear 'feminine,' even hyper-feminine. Her appearance is of one immersed in the line of descent, territorialized by established ideas and practices of the feminine. She was, like her older sister, noticeable for being more feminine than the other girls with her long blonde hair and frilly dresses. But when I came to the preschool on this particular visit, Francesca was engaged in a line of ascent that challenged the rigid boundaries of her category membership. She was, in Deleuzian terms, becoming different, not just entering a different category, but shaking the very structure of the categories she had been assigned. She was de-territorializing her own embodied sense of herself and, in doing so, was de-territorializing the categories masculine and feminine.

When I first noticed Francesca running through the forest with her short hair, blue jeans, and striped purple T-shirt, I mistook her for a boy. The teachers told me that Francesca's mother had caught her in the act of cutting off her beautiful hair and had been very upset. She had taken her to the hairdresser, who created a stylish, androgynous cut that made her look like a girl from one side and a boy from the other. On the day I first saw her, she also had on pink nail polish, but she no longer wore the frilly feminine dresses that had so visibly, along with her golden locks, marked her out as ultra-feminine.

Listening-as-usual, we might think of Francesca as naughty or rebellious, or even as wanting to be a boy. In other words she is in the category of girl first, and either she is deliberately or inadvertently getting her category membership wrong or she wants to be assigned to another category. In other words the entity of girl is recognized by her category. We understand what she does in terms of her category membership.

If we open up the space to emergent listening, then Francesca's cutting of her hair might be heard as a major *interference* in the category girl itself. The initial act of cutting could be read as a Bergsonian line of ascent into the not yet known. She had, in this way of listening, no way of knowing where she was going with it, though she may have had some notion that the cutting of her golden locks was to cut her apart from the princess-style femininity of her mother and sister. That may not have been an initiating factor leading to the cut *until* she encountered her mother's distress. The initiating moment may have been pure experiment—if I do this, what happens next?

The effect of the cut was, on the one hand, a reiteration of how prized the locks were and, on the other, a release from the categories she had been assigned to—girl-and-not-boy, and ultra-feminine-girl-and-not-tomboy. The second cut—in which Francesca, her mother, and the hairdresser were all involved—can be described as, in Barad's (2012b) terms, an agential cut: the cut was a "cutting together-apart" of the gender binary. The act of cutting by the hairdresser, at the instigation of the mother, involved cutting male and female together on Francesca's body. On one side at least she was still recognizably feminine.

The agency, in this act, in Barad's terms, lies not in the individual intentions of Francesca or her mother or the hairdresser, but in the event—the intra-action of all the entangled elements: these include, for example, a family in which princess-style femininity is valued; a school community that values strong girls; a preschool playground that provides space for girls to swing high on the swings, to scale giant rocks, and to find sticks to play with in the forest; the possibility that girls can wear jeans and T-shirts similar to the boys (where boys' clothes signify masculinity, courage, and strength); an available pair of scissors; a space that is private enough for the act of cutting to go briefly undetected; a history of mother-daughter encounters with the brushing and management of hair. All of these forces may have been at work to produce a playful/risky moment of hair-cutting, a line of ascent out of which emerged a creative resolution that brought male and female together on the same body.

The following week some teachers and I took a group of children on a picnic on top of a hill outside the preschool grounds. I wrote in my notes:

> On top of the hill teachers and children settle onto the mats the teachers have spread in a semi-circle and the teachers hand out drink and food. Together they point to things and talk about what they can see. Some children form pairs and talk to each other—Francesca with her best buddy Liam. Francesca talks and jokes with one of the teachers. Luke and 3 other boys play with their crusts, which have now become wild animals.

The picnic commences as an orderly, predictable teacher-directed event. The teachers encourage the children to talk in pairs, which they do, and Francesca engages one of the teachers in an amusing discussion. Then three boys shift the picnic in a playful direction, re-imagining the food they have been eating as transforming itself into another category—from food to wild animal. A teacher follows suit with her own playful category shifting, turning the water jar into a drum and initiating the singing of a song with some of the children. Then suddenly seven children swarm down the hill to explore a large broken branch. This turns into a game of running up the big hill and down again many times. They seem to know how far away they can go, and they mill at that invisible boundary on the hill-side of the footpath before running back up the hill again.

Then two girls burst over the boundary, across the path and into the field. A teacher goes after them and re-establishes the boundary of the picnic space. Crusts can become wild animals and jars can become drums, while the invisible boundary of the picnic space must be maintained. The relation between the predictable order that keeps everyone safe and the lines of ascent into the not-yet-known is carefully managed. While both girls and boys were running up and down the hill, a very strenuous activity requiring both strength and aerobic fitness, it was the girls who took the risk to try to extend the boundary. Trollet is not a place where girls are required to be the obedient ones in relation to the risk-taking boys. The teachers immediately re-assert the orderliness of the event by re-drawing the boundary-line. It is their job to keep the children safe at the same time as they work to open up imaginative experimental spaces for play. The children accept the re-drawing of the line and come back inside it and the boys immediately revive the wild animal play, and become wild animals:

> Three boys tumble together in a tangle of wrestling bodies. The bottom one squeals. The teacher intervenes to say the wrestling must stop. Four boys become a lion and some dragons. Liam is a lion chasing three other squealing boys into the forest and then out of the forest and down the hill. The squealing spreads to three other boys. Then the lion gets chased by two other boys. They land again in a wrestling tangle.

Once again the teacher re-creates order by disallowing the wrestling. The boys transform their game into wild chasing and then once again fall to wrestling. The teachers do not intervene again as it seems there is no-one being hurt. The orderliness of the picnic, in this moment, has been converted into an unpredictable line of ascent in which boys can become animals and engage in wrestling even though it has been forbidden. The wild-animal play appears to be self-evidently boys' play, and Francesca is not part of it.

Then Francesca opens up a new movement and the boys follow:

> Francesca goes alone to the forest and is playing with a stick. The boys join her. They run out of the forest with Francesca running out in front looking powerful with her stick. Francesca goes back into the forest alone with her stick and Liam runs after her.
>
> Just as rapidly as she takes the lead, she is alone again. When the boys take risks, when they risk a line of ascent, such as in their running with sticks through the forest with Francesca, *their risk-taking folds them out into the world as masculine*, since risk-taking is integral to masculinity. It is also true, at the same time, that their *recognition as masculine* is always at risk as they try out the new. The boy who was squealing at the bottom of the tangle of wrestling boys was not successfully accomplishing himself as masculine as he expressed his vulnerability and fear, for example.

In this particular moment of running after Francesca, the line of ascent involves running behind someone who is partly embodied as girl and partly embodied as boy. Is this act simply too risky in terms of securing one's identity as masculine?

When Francesca separates from the boys, she is joined by Liam and some girls. Liam is puffing from all the running. Then he needs to pee, so a teacher takes him over behind a tree. Francesca is now with three girls with sticks.

A lion comes over to the girls roaring, but no-one is scared, and they ignore him.

The children are in free flow here on multiple small lines of ascent. No-one knows what will happen next. It is an entanglement of emergent moments that cannot be made to make sense through strategies of listening-as-usual. Partly I am caught up in listening-as-usual myself as I resort to describing the children in terms of their gender category membership and their membership in the category children. At the same time I am intent on opening myself up to the multiple entangled movements of imagination, of power, and of shifting allegiances that make something new possible.

Next

Francesca is leading the other girl with a purple striped shirt through the forest. They both have sticks. Liam joins them with a stick and a plan! It is to be a war with guns. You must point the gun and yell *hey jo*.

But picnic time is over. Francesca is in the forest collecting sticks. A teacher tells her to pick up her jacket. Francesca says "never in my life" and looks at me as if to say "I know it's OK that you hold the jacket for me." I carry her jacket.

I am amused and charmed by her audacity, as I think are the teachers. But much more than this I am invited by her into a willingness to go with her in her experimentation with possible ways of being. At the same time I see/hear/feel a collective ambivalence about what she might be able to become in her encounters with others. How far can she go in her deconstruction of the categories she has been assigned, and when and how will they reclaim her? At one moment she embodies the possibility of becoming a leader of the boys, running with sticks through the forest with boys running behind her. But are they chasing her or following her? The game ends as rapidly as it begins. It seems her powerful moment has dissolved. But no, the girls are now collectively brave and not only are not afraid—or not willing to play at being afraid—of the roaring lion, but they completely ignore him as if he never roared. This is an extraordinarily powerful moment, albeit fleeting and entangled in multiple lines of force.

The securing of identity within the categorization of boy can never be flawless, but an endless engagement in small lines of ascent, risk-taking, territorializing the masculine body through a willingness to open themselves up to the not-yet-known of any particular movement or encounter—a doubled effect just as Deleuze and Bergson write about, territorializing and de-territorializing at the same time, endlessly differenciating in the very same acts through which they secure their identity within the social order as male.

Francesca's accomplishment of self, in contrast, has involved her in a tension between risk-taking (or de-territorializing lines of ascent) and the femininity desired for her by her mother. She runs fast through the forest with a stick, boys trailing after her, but is she leader of the boys or girl being pursued? Did the boys stop following her because they were ambivalent about following someone who was a girl, or half a girl, or were they momentarily uncertain whether she was the leader or the pursued? Did Francesca experience the same ambivalence?

Such ambivalence, in Barad's terms, *matters*; it is material, and its ethical implications *matter*. The children's play and its emergent intra-active folding with the gender order both reiterates the orderly gendered world and opens it up to the possibility of change, the possibility of differenciation / becoming different; these are changes that matter.

Conclusion

Emergent listening in this example positions me in one sense as a bystander, a listener open to the lines of ascent the children engage in and to their moments of becoming. I do not attempt to tell you the truth of what happened but offer a diffractive account in order to tease out some of the "entangled structure of the changing and contingent ontology of the world, including the ontology of knowing" (Barad, 2007, p. 73); I am also inevitably caught in listening-as-usual, caught in the categories through which we make the world fit into a particular order, divided into male and female, adult and child, normative and non-normative.

I have chosen a series of encounters through which a girl not only deconstructs the features that enable her to be read as ultra-feminine but opens up the possibility that the primacy of the *categories* gives way to the primacy of movement, where the movement itself comes before the identities—and deconstructs the categories themselves, even if only momentarily.

It may take some of you by surprise that I have not demonstrated emergent listening as an individual act that I have engaged in. It is not a method I am offering here. Rather it is an entangled movement that we have collectively accomplished: Francesca, the teachers, Francesca's mother, the hairdresser, you as reader, me as writer, the other children, the physical space of the playground, Deleuze, Barad, Bergson, and Nancy.

Emergent listening is vital for those of us interested in being open to difference. While we can't avoid listening-as-usual, not least because we depend on it, emergent listening enables us to approach life, and our encounters with others, as movement, as opening up ways of knowing and being that do not give primacy to category membership within the established social order.

Emergent listening involves being opened up from within and without (Nancy, 2007), and it involves a willingness to suspend judgment based on existing knowledge; it involves taking risks; it doesn't tie the other down in terms of their category memberships; it is ethical practice.

This is not ethics as a matter of separate individuals following a set of rules. Ethical practice, as both Barad and Deleuze define it, requires thinking beyond the already known, being open in the moment of the encounter, pausing at the threshold and crossing over. Ethical practice is emergent in encounters with others, in emergent listening with others. It is a matter of questioning what is being made to matter and how that mattering affects what it is possible to do and to think. Ethics is emergent in the intra-active encounters in which knowing, being, and doing (epistemology, ontology, and ethics) are inextricably entangled (Barad, 2007).

References

Barad, K. (2003). Posthumanist performativity: Toward an understanding of how matter comes to matter. *Signs. Journal of Women in Culture and Society, 28*(3), 801–831.

Barad, K. (2007). *Meeting the universe halfway: Quantum physics and the entanglement of matter and meaning.* Durham, NC: Duke University Press.

Barad, K. (2012a). Intra-actions. *Mousse Magazine, 34*, 76–81.

Barad, K. (2012b). Nature's queer performativity. *Kvinner Køn Forskning, 1–2*, 25–53.

Bennett, J. (2010). *Vibrant matter. A political ecology of things.* Durham, NC: Duke University Press.

Bergson, H. (1998). *Creative evolution.* Mineola, NY: Dover Publications Inc.

Davies, B. (2014). *Listening to children.* New York: Routledge.

Davies, B., & Gannon, S. (2009). *Pedagogical encounters.* New York: Peter Lang.

Deleuze, G. (1994). *Difference and repetition.* (Trans. P. Patton). New York: Columbia University Press.

Deleuze, G., & Guattari, F. (1987). *A thousand plateaus: Capitalism and schizophrenia*. London: Athlone Press.

Haraway, D. (1992). The promises of monsters: A regenerative politics for inappropriate/d others. In L. Grossberg, C. Nelson, & P. Treichler (Eds.), *Cultural studies* (pp. 295–337). New York: Routledge.

Malins, P. (2007). City folds: Injecting drug use and urban space. In A. Hickey-Moody & P. Malins (Eds.), *Deleuzian encounters: Studies in contemporary social issues* (pp. 151–168). Houndmills: Palgrave Macmillan.

Nancy, J.-L. (2007). *Listening*. (Trans. C. Mandell). New York: Fordham University Press.

6

QUEER AND QUARE AUTOETHNOGRAPHY

Robin M. Boylorn and Tony E. Adams

As researchers committed to personal narrative and social justice, we frequently use our experiences to identify abuses of power and instances of harm, offer accounts of marginal and silenced stories, and acknowledge and decenter our own positions of cultural privilege. To assist us with these commitments, we often rely on the aims and practices of queer theory, quare theory, and autoethnography—critical theoretical and methodological orientations that, when taken together, offer insights for using personal experience to describe abuses of power and tools for crafting evocative and accessible accounts of cultural life.

Although we have written separately about the productive relationships between queer theory and autoethnography (Adams & Holman Jones, 2008, 2011; Holman Jones & Adams, 2010, 2014) and quare theory and autoethnography (Boylorn, 2014; Johnson & Boylorn, 2015), we have not jointly or fully explored connections between queer theory, quare theory, and autoethnography—specifically, how autoethnography can enhance quare and queer research. In particular, we wonder: Who can be quare, and who can be queer? Which bodies are most at risk by trying to live queerly, or quarely, in social life? Can Robin, a black heterosexual woman raised in the rural Southern United States, ever be queer or do queer work? Can Tony, a white gay man raised in the rural Midwestern United States, ever use quare theory?

These questions guide us through this chapter. We first describe characteristics of quare theory and queer theory. We then describe autoethnography as a critical research method and discern productive relationships between queer theory, quare theory, and autoethnography. We conclude by offering a quare autoethnography and describe the difficulties in making it queer, and then offer a queer autoethnography and describe the difficulties in making it quare. As we demonstrate, autoethnography can ground queer theory—sometimes referred to as "high theory" (Adams & Holman Jones, 2011; Derbyshire, 1994)—in lived, concrete circumstances, as well as encourage queer theorists to better acknowledge intersectional understandings of personal experience. Autoethnography can also allow quare theory—sometimes referred to as "home theory" (Boylorn, 2014; Johnson, 2005)—to make better use of reflexivity and excel in its commitment to social justice.

Queer

"Queer" is a term with many uses. Queer can refer to same-sex attraction and/ or be used synonymously with "homosexual," "lesbian," "gay," or "bisexual" (Doty, 1993; Demory & Pullen, 2013); describe attempts to disrupt heterosexual—"heteronormative"—expectations of intimate relationships including biases against being single (Cobb, 2012), aspirations for marriage (Conrad, 2010), and assumptions about the importance of familial lineage and biological reproduction (Ahmed, 2006); define messages that rebel against culturally prevalent and insidious promises about optimism (Berlant, 2011), happiness (Ahmed, 2010), and the future (Dean, 2009); and/or refer to affects commonly perceived to be peculiar, inappropriate, incoherent, or disgusting—affects such as failure (Halberstam, 2011), depression (Cvetkovich, 2012), and melancholy (Holman Jones & Adams, 2014).

"Queer" can also be used as a verb. To queer social life requires vigilant attempts to disrupt erroneous assumptions about sexuality, rebel against heteronormative expectations, disassemble culturally prevalent and insidious promises, and/or reclaim affects commonly perceived to be problematic. To queer social life means challenging "unquestioned and taken-for-granted" ideas, identifying "underlying power relations," and offering "possibilities of resistance and other ways of thinking, doing, living, and loving" (Yep, 2013, p. 119). "Queer theory" is the area of research that investigates any of these uses of "queer," and being a good queer often means engaging in queer acts.

Although informed by lived experience, queer theory is critiqued for being too dense, abstract, and focused on "'single-variable' politics" (Johnson & Henderson, 2005, p. 5)—that is, too focused on issues of sexuality, desire, and/or decontextualized cultural values and affects rather than on the lived intersectionality of social identities, the contexts that inform harmful cultural values, and/or affects that are considered to be taboo. Queer theory can also promote a distrust of identity categories in its framing of identities as fluid and elusive, socially created fictions—a framing that dismisses the lived material experiences of how identities are understood, felt, and lived (Pérez, 2015). Further, given its use of "theory," queer theory also has been largely taken up in academic spaces rather than everyday contexts of oppression and is therefore seeped in race and class privilege (Marinucci, 2010).

Quare

E. Patrick Johnson (2005) describes quare as being "from the African American vernacular for queer; sometimes homophobic in usage, but always denot[ing] excess incapable of being contained within conventional categories of being"; and/or a "lesbian, gay, bisexual, or transgendered person of color who loves other men or women, sexually or nonsexually, and appreciates black culture and community"; and/or a person "committed to struggle against all forms of oppression" who understands that "sexual and gender identities always already intersect with racial subjectivity" (p. 125).

Borrowing Alice Walker's (1983) definition for womanism, which she developed in response to the unmistakable whiteness of feminism, Johnson's quare theory was in response to the unmistakable whiteness of queer theory, such as its inability to accommodate intersectional understandings of lived experience, the use of incomprehensible language, and its privileging of single-variable politics (e.g., focusing on oppression tied solely to sexuality and desire).[1] Johnson (2005) expands the definition of "queer" to include "meanings grounded in African American cultural rituals and lived experience" (p. 126) and, like Walker, specifies the cultural, classed, and raced context of a term that has long existed in the speech of black country folk and formally connects it to an intellectual tradition (Phillips, 2006). In other words, quare is inherently black, Southern, rural, and raced; conjures country folk and homegrown knowledge/s (Smith, 1983); and recognizes the heterogeneous experiences of people of color based on intersectionality.[2]

"Quare" can also be used as a verb. To quare "queer" is to acknowledge the epistemological circumstances of race- and class-based experiences (Johnson, 2005). To quare social life requires an appreciation, understanding, and/or critique of black culture (including homophobia); a resistance of white-washed notions of sexuality and desire; and an acknowledgement of different lived realities in culture-specific communities that both make room for and punish acts and performances perceived to be peculiar, inappropriate, incoherent, or disgusting. To quare social life means advocating for justice, highlighting, rather than dismissing, our differences, and understanding that race and class (always and inevitably) matter. "Quare theory" incorporates intersectionality, and being a good quare often means engaging in quare acts.

Queer and Quare Autoethnography

When understood as a critical method, autoethnography uses personal experience to describe and critique injurious cultural experiences, beliefs, and practices; identify weaknesses of existing research; and ascertain instances of injustice, privilege, and social harm. Critical autoethnography further encourages otherness, both an othering of the self and self-conscious reflection to empathize with the positionality of an identified other (Boylorn & Orbe, 2013). Autoethnographers accomplish these tasks by engaging in rigorous sense-making and meaning-making of confusing and contentious lived experiences, as well as through the use of reflexivity—that is, by explicitly acknowledging the ways in which their experiences and representations of those experiences are "partial, partisan, and problematic" (Goodall, 2000, p. 55). Further, through the limited use of jargon, technical language, various representational media (e.g., poetry, music), and storytelling devices such as plot, dialogue, and narrative voice, many autoethnographers also try to create evocative and accessible accounts of their experiences—accounts that disrupt the sterility of traditional social scientific research and accounts that can appeal to academic and non-academic audiences (Bochner & Ellis, 2016).

The critical aims and practices of autoethnography offer three primary ways queer and quare theory benefit from the method. First, although quare theory already values lived experience, queer theorists can use autoethnography to ground abstract, esoteric, and impractical concepts in lived, material circumstances. Second, with its use of rigorous sense-making and reflexivity, autoethnography encourages both queer and quare theorists to explicitly acknowledge their positions of marginalization as well as their limited perspectives and political commitments, identify the ways in which their representations enable and constrain others, and offer nuanced, intersectional understandings of personal experience. Third, even though quare theorists aim to create texts that can be used "on the front lines, in the trenches, on the street, or any place where the racialized and sexualized body is beaten, starved, fired, cursed" (Johnson, 2005, p. 129), queer and quare theoretical accounts[3]—many of those we cite, and even parts of this chapter—are often pierced with sterile and inaccessible prose. Autoethnography pushes queer and quare theorists to consider ways of becoming public intellectuals, particularly through the use of storytelling techniques, various representational media (e.g., blogs, poetry, music), and constructing texts that can appeal to academic and non-academic audiences.

Next, we show quare and queer autoethnography in practice. We first offer a quare tale and describe our (limited) attempts to make the tale queer. We then offer a queer tale and describe our (limited) attempts to make the tale quare. Although autoethnography can enhance the aims and practices of queer and quare theory, we also illustrate the ways in which queer theory and quare theory are incompatible.

Donnie Pig and Gertrude

When I (Robin) was barely old enough to understand the nuances of gender identity and performance, my father jokingly encouraged me to refer to my uncle as my aunt. I refused, not in resistance of the well-intentioned joke, but because there was no need for the announcement of a title before his name to reiterate our relationship. The eldest of my father's four brothers, Donnie Pig was my favorite. He was the uncle on my daddy's side I saw most often growing up, the one who made me feel special, the one who looked me in my eyes when he talked, the one who told me I was beautiful. I relished our time together and the way he talked to me like I was an adult, even when I was a child, and never ordered me out of rooms like everyone else. Unlike my other uncles, who would offer me distant greetings during intermittent visits, he would pat the seat right next to him, inviting me to lean in close so I could soak him up and absorb his goodness. I was drawn to him and unconsciously mirrored his mannerisms. To hear him tell it, I mocked the way he walked when I was a child, sashaying down the hall, switching and swaying my behind before I had one. He was an avid storyteller, telling lyrical lies and recounting memories in his nasal-toned falsetto voice, reenacting dialogue with precise detail, and describing events scene by scene with every family member within ear shot hanging on his every word, laughing out loud to every punchline.

I remember him bragging how he was a "bad bitch" when he cross-dressed and worked the streets of D.C. before I was born, before he moved back home to North Carolina to help take care of his bedridden mother, my grandmother. Donnie Pig, his nickname, was born a boy named Cleveland, though I didn't know what his real name was until I was 12 and came across a piece of mail with his birth name on it. "Who is Cleveland Jeffries?" I asked my father, wondering why he had a stranger's mail in his car.

"That's Donnie Pig's real name," my father responded, as if he was reminding me and not telling me for the first time about his brother's real name. It wasn't until I held that piece of mail in my hand that it occurred to me that Donnie Pig was not the kind of name my grandmother would have chosen for her first son, but Cleveland, as bold-sounding as the city in Ohio, seemed too hard and harsh a name for my effeminate effervescent favorite.

Donnie Pig was eccentric and unapologetically flamboyant. Even though I knew he wasn't a woman, in the sense that my mother and aunts were, he was proudly womanish, exaggerating his femininity through embodied deviance. He was a tall man and demanded attention when he walked in a room, only occasionally putting his hand on his hip, almost always exaggerating his bow-leggedness when he walked, his shoulders swaying rhythmically like he was dancing to a beat only he could hear. His high booty and twig-like legs always made him seem too young to be drinking a Mad Dog 20/20 and smoking a cigarette, which he always was. His long manicured nails were sometimes chipped or polished but were always on display as he threw his relaxed wrists around when he talked, eventually resting them on bony knees with his legs crossed. His pecan brown colored face held day-old peach fuzz, almond eyes, a subtle scar on his once-pierced nose, and a mole on the crease of his chin, like me. He favors my father, and I often wonder what he looks like as a woman. He sheepishly grins and unapologetically responds when kinfolk say, "Hey there gal!"

Black folk in the community where I grew up maliciously called men like my uncle "funny" or characterized them as having "some sugar in their tank."

I understood their words were insults for men who acted like women and who were sexually attracted to other men. No one in my family, who loved Donnie Pig, ever bothered to correct the bigoted comments. As a child, I didn't know how.

My maternal grandmother, Grandma Gert, was mannish and mean. A father-figure in a household without a father, she administered whoopings, cussings out, strict instructions, motherwit remedies, and second helpings of homemade meals she prepared after working 12-hour shifts. Her pre-arthritic hands were not for holding, and her deep voice was not delicate. She was not old, but she was grand. A mother of mothers with the demeanor of a man. She maintained a cool pose and scowl that made her always look mad even when she wasn't. Her smile was reserved for favored grandchildren and Saturday-night spades games, when brown liquor lingered on the bud of a lit cigarette held tightly between her lips. She wore men's jeans that were regularly dry cleaned, starched, and pressed, and she refused to carry a woman's purse, instead carrying a man's wallet (that held her money, driver's license, school pictures of grandchildren, and insurance card) in her right back pocket, which she called her "pocketbook." Her other back pocket held Salem cigarettes and a Bic lighter. On occasion, and at least one Sunday at church, she carried an unloaded Smith and Wesson in her bra. Everybody knew who she was and that she was not to be fucked with.

She liked to wear her slick hair with tight natural curls in a short cut with the edges close to the scalp so she went to a barber, never a beautician. With the exception of a white skirt suit she wore for a family portrait, I don't remember ever seeing my grandmother in a dress. She drank, she smoked, she cussed, she fought with her hands, and she was self-aware and deliberate about her actions. She was stingy with affection, only paying particular attention to me when I was sick or owed a spanking. She did all the things I was told were the bad habits of men. But because she was married, had five children, rotated lovers and special man friends, paid her bills and tithes on time, made homemade biscuits and gravy, and was quick-tempered and easy tongued, no one ever called her out of her name. No one ever speculated about her sexuality or accused her of loving women. When my cousin, aged five, asked our grandmother if she was a boy, she smacked her lips and said, "Hell nawl," and then went about her business, fixing breakfast plates.

Black folk in the community didn't seem to notice or make mention of my grandmother's proclivities. She wasn't called a bulldagger or dyke like city women accused of being "like that" or "trying to be men." She was never confronted or accused of being a bad mother, bad Christian, or undesirable woman. It was what it was, and she was who she was—a country black woman pinching pennies together and struggling to make sure ends would meet. Survival required masculinity. And her living it out was quare.

Donnie Pig and Gertrude are not actors with agency; they are characters in my autoethnography. They are quare subjects in my quare reading of my lived experience/s with them. Donnie Pig's queer identity, coupled with Gertrude's quare cultural upbringing, are points of analysis in my attempt at deconstructing the possibilities of quare autoethnography. While Donnie Pig's sexual and romantic preference for men influences his demeanor, his quareness is also connected to his rurality. My grandmother's quare performance of gender challenges false presumptions that gender identity is related to sexual identity or orientation, but it similarly reinforces the currency of black masculinity in black communities in the South. Her quare performance of authority, dominance, strength, and swagger gained her credibility and independence and protected her from public criticism.

A quare autoethnography of Donnie Pig and Gertrude privileges otherwise marginalized and silenced experiences and acknowledges Southern, black, non-gender-conforming identities. A quare reading also speaks to the fluidity of a woman's gender performance that is not afforded to men, especially black men. Although a queer reading would account for the relationship between identity and representation, it fails to consider the relevance and importance of cultural context and intersectionality.

I don't know if Donnie Pig and Gertrude would frame their experiences as quare or unique. However, I do know that they would not frame the experiences as queer. There are significant limitations of queer theory within the contexts of black (queer) lives (Johnson & Henderson, 2005). Because of religiosity and respectability, many of my home folk employ homophobic and heterosexist tendencies in their everyday lives and speech (Boylorn, 2014; Johnson, 2008). Influenced by generational and internalized racism and sexism, they are forced to negotiate the lesser of two perceived evils, in many instances reinforcing intolerance out of fear, ignorance, or both. Queer theory fails to acknowledge that black lived experience, and any critique thereof must move beyond language, performance, and power to account for the ways people of color are disenfranchised and marginalized by racism and classism (Cohen, 2005; Johnson, 2005). I recognize some of the sentiments within my family and community as problematic and homophobic (including, for example, my father's invitation for me to refer to my uncle as an aunt, and the ways my family consciously consumed and absorbed anti-gay rhetoric and slang within the community without speaking out/back, and the rigid gender script/performance required of black men, but not black women); quare theory offers language and praxis for loving critique.

As a child I did not have the language to challenge or fully understand the contradictory messages I received about quare identities, but I knew and understood that, even when queer black folk were maligned, they were still loved (Johnson, 2008). We did not throw each other away. Therefore, a quare intervention involves loving critique that respectfully subverts misconceptions and misunderstandings, while maintaining and protecting relationships. As a black woman academic and feminist with access to "high" theory, I try to queer quare, by calling out offensive comments and problematic language within and without the academy. Quare theory proposes a focused critique in the community in which I was raised and where I witnessed quare possibilities firsthand. Quare theory, unlike queer theory, emphasizes cultural and social critique within the context of homeplace (Johnson, 2005). In other words, while queer theory is situated within the academy, quare theory lives at home.

In my classroom, I can access the principles of queer theory and use them to disrupt problematic and normative notions of identity and gender—but the challenge is taking those impulses into the community. Homework, or taking theory to my mama's house, is not without complications. I don't actively police my community or consistently correct wrong thinking and problematic language, which would be a queer impulse. Instead, I strategically consider opportunities for intervention and improvement, honoring and recognizing my role in the community and the allegiances and relationships I have cultivated (e.g., black children are taught from a young age to "respect their elders"—a command that is consistent through adulthood—it is important to understand your position and role within the family and community, which occasionally requires biting one's tongue). Although quare theory insists that social and cultural critiques start and end at home, it recognizes the influence of oppression on the lives of the oppressed. Quare theory offers an imperfect and incomplete framework located in the communities and everyday experiences of quare folk of color.

Queer (White, Gay, Male) Bodies

10 p.m. Labor Day weekend in the United States. I (Tony) visit a bar that caters to lesbian, gay, bisexual, and queer customers. Tonight the bar hosts "Belly Rub Weekend" (BRW), an annual three-day excess eating and drinking event in Chicago that celebrates "chubs" (larger men), "gainers" (men who intentionally gain weight), "chasers" (men who admire chubs and gainers), "encouragers" (men who want to help men gain weight), and men who find chubs, gainers, and encouragers sexually attractive (Adams & Berry, 2013). On this evening, when many of the men greet and pass each other, I notice that they give "belly rubs": a subtle touch, or swipe, of others' bellies—a greeting, like a handshake, with a focus on the stomach.

"Are you a gainer or an encourager?" I am asked by some of the men—a question that, to me, suggests I am too small to be considered a chub yet, given my average physical build, might be someone who has gained, or wants to gain, weight.

"An encourager," I say. "Though I have gained about 40 pounds in the last few years."

An hour into the event, most of the men take off their shirts. Some of the men have small bellies and love handles; some of the men have muscled arms and large bellies; and some men weigh more than 400 pounds. Only a few of the men could be considered "thin." I would also classify most of the men in this space as white, though a few men seem to be Latino.

"Take off your shirt," one man says.

"Let your belly hang out!" another man yells.

I acquiesce and take off my shirt. I am nervous, as I think people are staring at my belly with disgust; I am used to moments when bigger weight is not encouraged and especially not celebrated, especially within the white gay male community—a community that tends to celebrate thin and fit bodies (Adams & Berry, 2013). But here, at this event, bellies are acknowledged and flaunted.

"I'm too thin," a man says to me as I order a beer. "No one pays me any attention."

I look at the (shirtless) man and gaze at his skinny frame. "You look great," I say. "But yes, you are much thinner than most of the men in the bar." I wonder about those moments outside of the event when he worries about being thin.

Throughout the night, men continue to rub bellies, expand bellies by chugging beer, remove belts, and unbutton (tight) pants. They also discuss numerous weight-gaining experiences and fantasies such as disregarding medical advice about expanding size; the swelling cost of food and clothing; the joys of not fitting in desks at school, chairs at the office or on airplanes, and booths in restaurants; worrisome comments made by friends and family members; and wanting to become immobile and bedbound, all the while being fed by an encouraging boyfriend.

As a gay man who frets about gaining weight and who finds bigger men sexually attractive, I celebrate this event and the attendees' talk. I rarely hear about weight and size being celebrated, and, in everyday contexts, I am bombarded by assumptions that thin and fit bodies are more desirable and attractive. As such, I understand this event and these men as queer: They offer alternative ways of living and being in the world (Yep, 2013, p. 119); disrupt culturally prevalent ideas about size and sexual attractiveness, especially the thin and fit gay male aesthetic (Berry, 2007; Whitesel, 2014); and advocate beliefs and practices that others might find to be wrong.

However, if I try to use quare theory to understand the event and these men, I encounter some obstacles. For example, if quare theory values intersectional understandings of lived experience, can I offer an adequate understanding of intersectionality, escape my whiteness or my maleness, or ever know about how it feels like to be a "lesbian, gay, bisexual, or transgendered person of color" (Johnson, 2005, p. 125)? No. I can only speculate about how a person of color might experience the event; speculate about what it means, and how it feels, to be a non-white body in the predominantly white space; speculate about the microaggressions—those subtle, covert, and seemingly innocent slights—that persons who do not pass as white might experience. I also note that such speculation can be condescending, dangerous, and an act always already stained with the (white, gay, male) privilege of being able to maneuver the event with ease.

In my attempt to be quare, I can turn to others who have written about race, sexuality, and attraction and think about the possible ways racism and sexism exist at the event. For example, I think about Dawson's (2015) writing about his experiences as a black gay man who has gone on dates with white gay men—those times when white gay men claim to want "BBC" (big black cock) or "Blk [black] ass"; or when they ask about the size of his penis; or when they offer him money for sex. Dawson changed his dating profile to ask (white) men not to make such comments and, in response, offended some white men yet received praise from men of color. Dawson even noted that although men of color "receive messages online for sex by white guys," they are often ignored at predominantly white bars and "overlooked by bartenders." Would the white men at BRW treat black men in these ways? Would bartenders overlook black bodies?

I also think about Eguchi's (2014) writings about race, sexuality, and hegemonic masculinity, and how particular bodies, especially gay Asian bodies, may be perceived as feminine, submissive, and secondary to "straight-acting" white bodies. Like Dawson, Eguchi describes disparaging interactions with white gay men as well as the difficult times ordering "drinks from the White bartenders," how these bartenders have treated him as a "stupid foreigner," and how "bartenders of color" never treated him in such degrading ways (p. 281). I wonder if the (white) BRW bartenders would overlook Asian bodies or treat them as stupid foreigners? Or would the BRW men—men who desire bigger and fatter bodies—respect "skinny little Asian bodies" (p. 280)? I can only speculate: I assume many BRW men would disregard skinny men, unless the skinny men desired bigger bodies, but I do not know if the bartenders would disregard bodies that did not pass as white—an acknowledgement of ignorance as I cannot escape my white body, and an observation about whiteness in that I may never recognize if and when a bartender has mistreated me because of my race.

Although I have offered a limited discussion of race and sexuality, I am even more speculative about how a body perceived as female or transgender might experience BRW. I have attended BRW for two years, and I observed only cismen (or people who pass as cismen) attend the event; to my knowledge (or ignorance!), no ciswomen were ever present. I also cannot effectively understand the classed aspects of the event, only to note that men most likely learned about BRW via an online community of chubs, gainers, chasers, encouragers, and admirers and, as such, had to access, and know how to use, a computer or a Web-enabled device. Further, once at BRW, attendees need excess money to spend on alcohol or have the social capital (e.g., attractive appearance, relational skills, and being perceived as white, male, able-bodied, etc.) to flirt with men who might buy them a drink.

I also wonder about the privileges of being able to obtain a bigger size and still be able to maneuver social interaction with ease. More specifically, which bodies can gain 50 pounds easily, without severe judgment or consequences, and without the weight gain being attributed to their race, gender, or character?

As a white man, I speculate that I could gain 50 pounds without receiving too much critique; I assume that I am able to expand more safely compared to white women who gain the same amount of weight and who are often held to unattainable and unhealthy standards of thinness. I think about the recent celebrations of "dad bods"—that is, (heterosexual, white) men who gain weight after fathering a child and who no longer worry about maintaining a thin and fit physique. Are "mom bods" equally celebrated? I also speculate that I can gain weight without having to worry about how my size reflects on my race, of being perceived as unhealthy or gluttonous or as failing to maintain a "skinny little Asian" body (Eguchi, 2014, p. 280).

BRW espouses queer sensibilities in that it disrupts norms of body size, desire, and sexuality, and I can use queer theory to offer important insights about the event, especially for anyone (only men?) interested in celebrating bigger, expanding bodies. However, queer theory—with its lack of, and inability to effectively consider, intersectionality—also grants me the privilege to not think about who can (not) be queer and what being queer costs in terms of social privilege; I can avoid thinking about how BRW may perpetuate harmful goals of consumption, perpetuate norms of inclusion and exclusion, and possibly even promote racist, misogynistic, and classist desires. As such, I turn to quare theory to help with intersectionality, yet I get stuck in speculation, unable to effectively describe how the event is lived by bodies that are not white, gay, or male (or even middle-class, urban, able-bodied, etc.). I am able to offer a queer account but not a quare account, and I am unable to make my queer account quare.

Conclusion

Queer theory and quare theory promote productive conversations about power, privilege, and social justice. Queer theory is most productive for disrupting heteronormative expectations of intimate relationships; rebelling against cultural expectations tied to sexuality and desire; reclaiming peculiar, inappropriate, incoherent, and disgusting affects; and offering new possibilities of "thinking, doing, living, and loving" (Yep, 2013, p. 119). Quare theory is most productive for resisting white-washed notions of sexuality and desire, offering homegrown knowledges and appreciations of black culture, illustrating the necessity of intersectionality, and acknowledging our communal relationships and allegiances.[4]

Autoethnography can also help quare and queer theorists excel with these commitments. Queer theorists can use autoethnography to ground abstract, esoteric, and impractical concepts in lived, material circumstances. Queer and quare theorists can use autoethnography to explicitly acknowledge their limited perspectives and political commitments, identify the ways in which their representations enable and constrain others, offer intersectional understandings of personal experience, and construct texts that can appeal to academic and non-academic audiences.

However, in doing queer and quare autoethnography, we realized lived experience is not translatable: Robin couldn't queer and Tony couldn't quare. When Robin tried to queer her story, it wasn't white enough. When Tony tried to quare his story, it was too white, too male, and too focused on sexuality. Further, Robin had to think about how she identifies with quareness because of her Southern rural upbringing and as an ally, not because of her sexual identification; and Tony had to consider the privileges that come with being able to live in queer ways and wanting to disturb the (cultural) peace in terms of body size, sexuality, and desire.

But we can turn these limitations into productive lessons. Robin can use queer theory to fuck with gender, sexuality, and desire, to identify as heterosexual yet also find ways to critique heterosexism and participate in queer activism in her home communities. Tony can use quare theory to acknowledge the significance of intersectionality yet also refuse to appropriate quareness as his own (a white act!), recognizing he is able to speculate only about how it may feel to be a queer person of color traversing predominantly white spaces—especially those high academic spaces—in which he dwells.

Borrowing words from Cohen (2005), "[we] would suggest that it is the multiplicity and interconnectedness of our identities that provide the most promising avenue for the destabilization and radical politicalization of these same categories" (p. 45). Together, we can engage queer and quare autoethnography to continue our commitment to inclusivity and social justice, deconstruct and decenter our own positions of privilege, and make space for maligned and silenced stories and representations.

Notes

1 As Johnson (2005) writes, "Some queer activist groups . . . have argued fervently for the disavowal of any alliance with heterosexuals, a disavowal that those of us who belong to communities of color cannot necessarily afford to make" (p. 130).

2 See Cooper's (2015) article for an explanation of intersectionality as an account of power, not personal identity. Cooper argues that intersectionality is about not race, class, and sex but about racism, classism, and sexism.

3 In response to Johnson's quare theory, Lee (2003) offers "kuaer theory" to represent race consciousness, womanism, and transnationalism. She embraces quare theory but proposes a further departure to represent her personal account and a critique of intersectionality.

4 Johnson (2005) states, "[Q]uare studies offers a more utilitarian theory of identity politics, focusing not just on performers and effects, but also on contexts and historical situatedness. . . . Quare studies grants space for marginalized individuals to enact 'radical black subjectivity,' by adopting the both/and posture of 'disidentification.' Quare studies proposes a theory grounded in a critique of essentialism and an enactment of political praxis" (p. 141).

References

Adams, T. E., & Berry, K. (2013). Size matters: Performing (il)logical male bodies on Fat-Club.com. *Text and Performance Quarterly, 33*(4), 308–325.

Adams, T. E., & Holman Jones, S. (2008). Autoethnography is queer. In N. K. Denzin, Y. S. Lincoln, & L. T. Smith (Eds.), *Handbook of critical and indigenous methodologies* (pp. 373–390). Thousand Oaks, CA: Sage.

Adams, T. E., & Holman Jones, S. (2011). Telling stories: Reflexivity, queer theory, and autoethnography. *Cultural Studies <=> Critical Methodologies, 11*(2), 108–116.

Ahmed, S. (2006). *Queer phenomenology: Orientations, objects, others.* Durham, NC: Duke University Press.

Ahmed, S. (2010). *The promise of happiness.* Durham, NC: Duke University Press.

Berlant, L. (2011). *Cruel optimism.* Durham, NC: Duke University Press.

Berry, K. (2007). Embracing the catastrophe: Gay body seeks acceptance. *Qualitative Inquiry, 13,* 259–281.

Bochner, A. P., & Ellis, C. (2016). *Evocative autoethnography: Writing lives and telling stories.* Walnut Creek, CA: Left Coast Press.

Boylorn, R. M. (2014). From here to there: How to use auto/ethnography to bridge difference. *International Review of Qualitative Research, 7*(3), 314–326.

Boylorn, R. M., & Orbe, M. P. (Eds.) (2013). *Critical autoethnography: Intersecting cultural identities in everyday life.* Walnut Creek, CA: Left Coast Press.

Cobb, M. (2012). *Single: Arguments for the uncoupled.* New York: New York University Press.

Cohen, C. J. (2005). Punks, bulldaggers, and welfare queens: The radical potential of queer politics? In E. P. Johnson & M. G. Henderson (Eds.), *Black queer studies: A critical anthology* (pp. 21–51). Durham, NC: Duke University Press.

Conrad, R. (2010). *Against equality: Queer critiques of gay marriage.* Lewiston, ME: Against Equality Publishing Collective.

Cooper, B. (2015). Intersectionality. In L. Disch & M. Hawkesworth (Eds.), *The Oxford handbook of feminist theory* (pp. 385–406). New York: Oxford University Press.

Cvetkovich, A. (2012). *Depression: A public feeling.* Durham, NC: Duke University Press.

Dawson, L. (2015, June 13). Dear white gay men: Stop objectifying gay men of color. *Huffington Post.* Accessed December 1, 2015 from http://www.huffingtonpost.com/lamar-dawson/dear-white-gay-men-stop-o_b_7777276.html.

Dean, T. (2009). *Unlimited intimacy: Reflections on the subculture of barebacking.* Chicago: University of Chicago Press.

Demory, P., & Pullen, C. (Eds.) (2013). *Queer love in film and television: Critical essays.* New York: Palgrave Macmillan.

Derbyshire, P. (1994). A measure of queer. *Critical Quarterly, 36,* 39–45.

Doty, A. (1993). *Making things perfectly queer: Interpreting mass culture.* Minneapolis: University of Minnesota Press.

Eguchi, S. (2014). Disidentifications from the West(ern): An autoethnography of becoming an other. *Cultural Studies <=> Critical Methodologies, 14*(3), 279–285.

Goodall, H. L. (2000). *Writing the new ethnography.* Walnut Creek, CA: AltaMira Press.

Halberstam, J. (2011). *The queer art of failure.* Durham, NC: Duke University Press.

Holman Jones, S., & Adams, T. E. (2010). Autoethnography and queer theory: Making possibilities. In N. K. Denzin & M. G. Giardina (Eds.), *Qualitative inquiry and human rights* (pp. 136–157). Walnut Creek, CA: Left Coast Press.

Holman Jones, S., & Adams, T. E. (2014). Undoing the alphabet: A queer fugue on grief and forgiveness. *Cultural Studies <=> Critical Methodologies, 14*(2), 102–110.

Johnson, A. L., & Boylorn, R. M. (2015). Digital media and the politics of intersectional queer hyper/in/visibility in between women. *Liminalities: A Journal of Performance Studies, 11*(1), 1–26.

Johnson, E. P. (2005). 'Quare' studies, or (almost) everything I know about queer studies I learned from my grandmother. In E. P. Johnson & M. G. Henderson (Eds.), *Black queer studies: A critical anthology* (pp. 124–157). Durham, NC: Duke University Press.

Johnson, E. P. (2008). *Sweet tea: Black gay men of the south*. Chapel Hill, NC: University of North Carolina Press.

Johnson, E. P., & Henderson, M. G. (2005). Introduction: Queering black studies/'quaring' queer studies. In E. P. Johnson & M. G. Henderson (Eds.), *Black queer studies* (pp. 1–17). Durham, NC: Duke University Press.

Lee, W. (2003). Kuaering queer theory: My autocritography and a race-conscious, womanist, transnational turn. *Journal of Homosexuality, 45*(2–4), 147–170.

Marinucci, M. (2010). *Feminism is queer: The intimate connection between queer and feminist theory*. New York: Zed Books.

Pérez, H. (2015). *A taste for brown bodies: Gay modernity and cosmopolitan desire*. New York: New York University Press.

Phillips, L. (Ed.) (2006). *The womanist reader*. New York: Routledge.

Smith, B. (Ed.) (1983). *Home girls: A Black feminist anthology*. New York: Kitchen Table: Women of Color Press.

Walker, A. (1983). *In search of our mothers' gardens: Womanist prose*. San Diego: Harcourt Brace Jovanovich.

Whitesel, J. (2014). *Fat gay men: Girth, mirth, and the politics of stigma*. New York: New York University Press.

Yep, G. A. (2013). Queering/quaring/kauering/crippin'/transing 'other bodies' in intercultural communication. *Journal of International and Intercultural Communication, 6*(2), 118–126.

7

THIS IS NOT A COLLABORATIVE WRITING

Mirka Koro-Ljungberg and Jasmine B. Ulmer

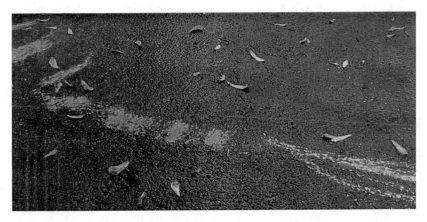

FIGURE 7.1   Untitled 1

Koro-Ljungberg, Hendricks, & Ulmer, 2014

> *Wet asphalt, leaves, chalk, lines, cracks, dirt, blended materials, colors, and textures write. How can one write (collaboratively) in the absence of authors, writers, scholars, inquirers, collaborators, and collaboration itself?*
>
> One writes. One writes alone. One writes with and without. Nobody writes and all write. This is not a collaborative writing.

Maybe this text complicates writing as a fixed and normative scholarly practice. Maybe it problematizes premeditated and co-constructed textual production. Maybe it refuses the always already existing possibility for (collaborative) writing while engaging different materials in various (un/non)writing contexts. Maybe it is time to acknowledge presence and absence in the collaborative construction of visual writing (see Ulmer & Koro-Ljungberg, 2015). Maybe this project builds from other collaborative and experimental projects, projects that extend various forms of academic writing, including the work of Bridges-Rhoads and Van Cleave (2014); Gale and Wyatt (2009); Hofsess and Sonenberg (2013); Guttorm, Hilton, Jonsdottir, Löytönen, McKenzie, Gale, and Wyatt (2013); Löytönen, Koro-Ljungberg, Carlson, Orange, and Cruz (2015); and Wyatt, Gale, Gannon, and Davies (2010, 2011).

As we may be celebrating more generative and organic forms of scholarly writing, we also are preparing for the funeral of collaborative humanistic and anthropocentric writings. In current virtual and nomadic worlds, writing, writers, and collaboration take different and unanticipated forms including anti- or post-human extensions. By acknowledging these organic and potentially 'life-like' forms of writing, we also aim for the mummification of shared thoughts and mutually co-constructed text. We wonder how one can engage in collaborative writing if the words, ideas, images, or concepts are problematized and they belong to nobody or everybody all at once.

In other words, this is not a collaborative writing.

Rather, this writing is an experiment that extends and challenges rather than confirms or builds. This writing gets its energy from departures, and it operates through surprise, movement, and the unexpected (see also Deleuze & Guattari, 1987; Massumi, 2002). The writing is not collaborative, peaceful, univocal, or textual. This writing is not. When writing seems to happen, it appears as events, stutters, flows, diversifications, or fragments. Writing in absence while tracing the others and attempting to run from oneself. Writing does not represent or speak about something, but it is 'something,' and it might function as everything (see Hannula, Suoranta, & Vaden, 2014). As we write, we neglect and object to the label 'collaborative writing' in the hopes that the language used here might hide our potential collaboration and any possible presence of co-construction. As Foucault (1998) writes, "language can and must cover up everything; it is never quiet, since it is in the living economy of situations, their visible nervure" (p. 56).

This imagined yet potentially covered up collaborative writing is merely a similitude referring to nothing except maybe to the absence of collaborative writing itself. We transfer texts and images in such a way that they could be read as forms of collaborative writing, but they are not. We make writing mistakes-on-purpose (see Keane, 2015) by misleading, breaking, erasing, and confusing, and we write one while thinking two. In this context, collaborative writing is divorced from its name and practice (or that is what we propose without making any truth claims and arguments to be validated). This is a text that could describe collaborative writing, but the writing or collaborative writing herein resembles collaborative writing that is not. Returning to Foucault (1998), "writing unfolds like a game that . . . invariably goes beyond its own rules and transgresses its limits" (p. 206). The point of writing might be to create a space where writing can disappear and writers are reduced to the singularity of their absence.

Because writing might be absent or unanticipated, no one knows what or where or how writing may occur. These are interactions inspired by Deleuze, Derrida, Foucault, and Barthes gone wrong. An experience of a loss of the author and a loss of oneself multiplied by two. Writing without a plan happens, this virtual event surprises the writers themselves, and many tiny voices within the writers get disturbed. Writing appears almost the same but not quite. Scratch that. Writing almost never feels the same. Scratch that. Many writers writing in the same space, colliding. Sometimes. Never really. No, this is not a collaborative writing.

AND

We find that our version of (not so) collaborative writing is prompted by unfamiliar text, images, and examples that appeared on the page since the last writing and individual interactions with this text. In many ways the past writing of each and use of the other refuses or denies itself and makes oneself unrecognizable. Some text and images resonate; some silently become invisible or inaccessible. One writes afresh, remembering and inspired, yet the collaborative writing stays refused, sidetracked, bypassed, and amodal. Knowing and writing become entangled and inseparable.

AND

New writing events emanate from a writing experiment. This is a first but not the first. But this is not the beginning since there is no beginning to this (collaborative writing) project. Ideas have emerged and continue to emerge. First ideas come and go. As soon as the first appears, another first lurks behind and waits for its turn. Some get materialized and written about, yet always only partially. Some are buried and forgotten, but they get reborn in other writings or in the images of others. Others emerge in the form of dreams, imaginary conversations, or previous writings undone.

In the past we have (re)produced images as objects and then (re)produced objects as images. But these are not new collaborative writings or images, either. We wrote about repetition in the past, and we wrote with the repetition from the past. We wrote with lines of stutter, reverse, and jamming (figure 7.2). We wrote with images as vital illusion (figure 7.3). We wrote through cartography (figure 7.4). Now we return to lines. Lines without an author, scholarship without a researcher, and the impossibilities of writing together and on our own.

FIGURE 7.2 Untitled 1

Koro-Ljungberg, Hendricks, & Ulmer, 2014

FIGURE 7.3 Untitled 2

Koro-Ljungberg & Ulmer, 2015

FIGURE 7.4 Untitled 3

Ulmer & Koro-Ljungberg, 2015

Barthes (2012) was delighted by words because of "the formulation which brings them together, not because of their own power or beauty" (p. 45). Can one, the other, and the one again write in the style that is in itself an absence of the style? How can writing be a sea in which the potential authors must learn to swim? Writing does not deliver messages inasmuch as it functions as a message. Messages still seem impossible. Scratch Barthes. This cannot be collaborative writing.

————————————————ABSENCE————————————————

Writing Obsessed With Its Own Definition(s)

Collaborative writing does and produces, becoming possible in its own changing definitions. We now rotate through a series of potential definitions—turning collaborative writing forward and backward, upside-down, sideways, and this way and that. In the process, we explore collaborative writing from a variety of angles: what it is; where it occurs; how it writes into and within; who it writes with and at; what it writes toward, by, and as; and if it is even written, much less read. By diffracting (Barad, 2007) potential elements of collaborative writing through a definitional kaleidoscope, we continue to problematize co-constructed textual production. The possibilities of collaborative writing (nots) are indeed many.

Collaborative writing occurs at the intersections of the accidental and theoretical. One writes with theories and theorists (see Wyatt et al., 2011; Jackson & Mazzei, 2012), but only in accidental ways. Barthes (2012), for example, promotes *writing degree zero*—writing obsessed with its own definition and whose task is to impose something beyond language and signs. Writing degree zero signifies an absence of style, commitment to linguistic rules or genres, and maybe the death of an author. This kind of writing avoids contamination, and it says more than is 'true' while appearing to be honest. Our attempts to create collaborative writing-nots come back and return to us as forms of fabricated collaborative writing. Writing degree zero calls for continuously adaptable engagement with different forms of writing, such as when Magritte and Foucault (1998) write the difference between representation and being. Derrida (1987), moreover, writes to a nameless audience through a series of *envois*—a series of one-directional letters that may not arrive at their intended destination. The possibilities of transmission and receipt remain tenuous. It is only when communications are 'intercepted' that an exchange might occur. This (un)collaborative writing draws from them all. Or not.

Collaborative writing writes into the void through Derrida, who does not respond to directionality or assumed responses. Instead Derrida (1987) suggests,

It is always a question of setting (something) on its way/voice [*voix*], and alley oop, by pressing on a well-paced lever, to compel unplugging, derailing, hanging up, playing with the switch points and sending off elsewhere, setting it off route (go to see elsewhere if I am there: and someone is always found there, to carry on, to take up the thread of the story, you follow).

(pp. 160–161)

Like a baton relay that has expanded without direction beyond the closed-circuit track, collaborative writing forms a possible exchange—a possible 'interception' of communication. Each communication potentially moves and takes off along its own line of flight (Deleuze & Guattari, 1987), carried by others in unforeseen directions. Or not.

Collaborative writing may happen by refusal and stoppage and consequent multiplication. How many times has this writing refused itself, sidetracked itself, bypassed itself? Writing paralyzed (Bridges-Rhoads, 2015) by itself. Collaborative writing by starting and stopping. And in the starts and stops, trying to remember not so much what was written, but which of our versions happened to be writing. Deleuze and Guattari offer that "[s]ince each of us was several, there was already quite a crowd," and soon thereafter found themselves at a juncture in the text "where it is no longer of any importance where one says I. We are no longer ourselves. Each will know his own. We have been aided, inspired, multiplied" (1987, p. 3). Collaborative writing by multiplication. Collaborative writing by (n + 1) (infinitely many).

Collaborative writing could be as much an issue of multiplication as it is its inverse operation: division. Deleuze, for example, might also describe the divisibility of collaborative writing. As he posits,

> Individuation is mobile, strangely supple, fortuitous and endowed with fringes and margins; all because the intensities which contribute to it communicate with each other, envelop other intensities and are in turn enveloped. The individual is far from indivisible, never ceasing to divide and change its nature.
>
> *(Deleuze, 1994, p. 257)*

Collaborative writing is much the same: Collaborative writing divides itself, and we divide ourselves as (un)collaborative writers. Division, multiplication. Multiplication, division. Remind us, what is writing whom is writing what again?

Collaboratively writing with others problematizes notions of singular, stable identity. Collaborative writers write alone and together at the same time; they exist within the same space as many writing one. They continuously write atop the peeling, flaking layers of other writings as they write atop themselves (figure 7.5). The most recent version of the text then asserts itself to become the most visible of the writings and, in the process, renders previous versions partial, invisible, indecipherable, and/or covered in the past. Previous images of writing petrify these fleeting moments. Though writers often write alone, what is produced forms an unintentional collaboration.

FIGURE 7.5   ADVENTURE TIME with candy girl

J. Ulmer, 2015, Detroit

As Deleuze (1995) might suggest, "even when you think you're writing on your own, you're always doing it with someone else you can't always name" (p. 141). Other recent examples include troubling the (im)possibility of single authorship (Van Cleave & Bridges-Rhoads, 2013); writing with the ghosts of other scholars (Koro-Ljungberg, 2016); and writing and dialoguing alongside imaginary versions of philosophers (in Hendricks, 2015; see also Brkich & Barko, 2012).

Collaborative writing thus might involve collaborating with imaginary figures, even if collaboration is an imitation of something that is always already lost. For instance, if we were to ask philosophers how to respond to the question of what (un)collaborative writing might be, possible imaginary responses might include the following:

BARTHES: (Un)collaborative writing is "the negative where all identity is lost, starting with the very identity of the body writing" (1977, p. 142).

DERRIDA: What is writing? Where is writing (1976)?

MALABOU: Writing is at its dusk (2010)—

BARTHES: (Un)collaborative writing is a "tissue of quotations" (1977, (p. 146), especially given that "the book itself is only a tissue of signs, an imitation that is lost, infinitely deferred" (p. 147).

DERRIDA (CITING LEVI-STRAUSS): Collaborative writing, (un)collaborative writing . . . "Only similar things can differ, and only different things can be similar" (Derrida & Weber, 1995, p. 156).

DELEUZE AND GUATTARI: What does it matter? "Write to the nth power, the n—1 power. . . . Don't be one or multiple, be multiplicities!"

(1987, p. 24, emphasis in original)

Just as collaborative writing is marked by imagination and multiplicities, collaborative writing also might also be constituted in additive singularity. Bourassa (2002) proposed that language and literature enclose singularities and are "partial realizations of singularity-events" (p. 70) themselves. He continues, writing that novels and writing do not represent humanity even though they are concerned with the human. In contrast, novels, texts, humanity, and their surroundings potentially are constituted "in the vicinity of the same set or series of singularities" (p. 70). When crossing over between these singularities and outside where the singularities happen, novels, texts, and humans appear as non-personal and non-subjective. By approaching (un)collaborative writing as constituted in singularity, each piece of writing could be seen as additive over time. Perhaps this is collaborative writing by a sequence of partial sums in which S_n never quite equals $X_0 + X_1 + \ldots X_n$.

Or collaborative writing occurs when *writing-thoughts join writing-bodies* to produce intra-active, collaborative text—a collaborative version of choreographic writing (Ulmer, 2015) in which uncontained words extend beyond standard typeface lettering into somatic being and movement. A collaborative writing with theoretical and methodological irruptions, and a writing that explodes alongside theoretical and methodological irruptions as none, one, two, three, and more embodied writer-dancers move words. Choreographic writing is, within new materialist frames, an intra-active form of writing. For Barad (2007), intra-action signifies *"the mutual constitution of objects and agencies of observation within phenomena"* (p. 197, emphasis in original) and exists in direct "contrast to 'interaction,' which assumes the prior existence of distinct entities" (p. 197). If the mind and body intra-actively fuse together in choreographic collaborative writing, then what might happen if the mind and body joined the natural environment in other forms of (collaborative) new materialist writing? New materialist collaborative writings might involve mixed-media entanglements of words, textures, materials, technologies, and natural settings. Put differently, post-human sand, dirt, sticks, trees, rocks, grass, and shells might join us in multi-authored writing collaborations.

Collaborative writing within new materialist theories might vary and continue to take unexpected forms. To illustrate, perhaps in new materialist frameworks, writers do not write

FIGURE 7.6   Untitled 4

Koro-Ljungberg, 2015

but writers are

FIGURE 7.7   Untitled 5

Koro-Ljungberg, 2015

the cracks in texts, relations, material encounters
as new materialist (collaborative) writers

FIGURE 7.8 Untitled 6

Koro-Ljungberg, 2015

intra-act with the surrounding environment in material-discursive collaborations. Nature collaborates.

Technology collaborates AND new actors

FIGURE 7.9 Untitled 7

Koro-Ljungberg, 2015

new collaborators emerge as writers.

Collaboratively writing with others might further involve images as collaborators. For instance, online photographers offer images with broad licenses so that their written images may travel at will; in using these images, photographs may join collaborative writing projects. They write images, we write with images, images write themselves. Rocks, sand, and cracks elsewhere continue to write.

FIGURE 7.10   Mudracks Along the Shoreline of Storr's Lake (San Salvador Island, Bahamas)

St. John, 2013

FIGURE 7.11   Sand

Sputzer, 2011

FIGURE 7.12   Borderland Construction, 1921 – Tucson, Arizona.

Sableman, 2010

Or perhaps it is collaborative writing if the reader is not lost and audience has not disappeared.

Still Not a

René Magritte's painting and essay *This Is Not a Pipe* prompted Foucault (1998) to elaborate on the difference between being and representation. The mismatch between ontological positioning and the reproduction of that same positioning is hindered by delay, representational gaps, and distancing. Similarly, collaborative writing as written here does not represent our writing events, writer selves, marks of ink on the paper, or even words written in the sand. Like Magritte, we are naming something that does not need to be named because the form of collaborative writing is too well known and familiar. And by naming this writing's 'image' as collaborative, we deny this collaborative writing its "collaborativeness and writingness."

By naming this text as not a collaborative writing, we create an illusive separation of the image of writing / writing experience from itself. By doing so, we hope to set collaborative writing floating "whether near or apart from itself, whether similar to or unlike itself, no one knows" (Foucault, 1998, p. 197). For Foucault, it is also a question of freeing painting (or experience/event/sense of collaborative writing) from resemblance and affirmation. Foucault suggests that this could be done by disrupting bonds between resemblance and affirmation (or image and text), bringing one into play without the other, generating the continuation of the similar into the infinity without affirming these continuations as the one (to be represented).

Following Foucault, we propose that none of this is a form of collaborative writing, but rather it is a text that may simulate collaborative writing, an image of collaborative writing that simulates the image, a collaborative writing that resembles a collaborative writing-not (figure 7.13). Collaborative writing-nots might assume other forms, including (un)collaborative dream writings, almost collaborative mo(ve)ments (Davies & Gannon, 2006), and the undoing of previously collaborative writings. These are all potential versions of collaborative writing-nots. Maybe.

FIGURE 7.13 This is Not a Pipe (This Title is a Ripoff from Michel Foucault)

Pederson, 2006

A Collaborative Writing Not

These words used to be a collaborative writing (Ulmer & Koro-Ljungberg, 2015). Now they are not. Undeleted words are the same—only shifted.

think in talk more for   two monologues   wherever, importance
this paper do need to
    cartography and its Emerging in a sense. I we do cartography as a methodology.
How occasionally I was thinking that betweeness-gap in me and you?   Dialogue
occasionally intersects. Or overlaps. Or not. Whenever. General methodological
utterances   Yes—I agree   no—you don't.

No, this is not a collaborative writing. A collaborative writing made un-collaborative.

(Un)collaboratively Dream-Writing Alone

4:22 a.m.

I am awakened by tiny songbirds protesting the wind, the cold, and the impending arrival of winter. From their refuge on the ledge between the fourth and fifth floors, from their sparse protection behind a single pine tree, they announce their displeasure. I reach for the extra blankets I have kicked off during the night. I am cold now, too, but the birds soon awaken the heater. *What is collaborative writing?* I wonder, as their choral protestations fade into the background hum and the creeping warmth.

I dream of collaborative writing. I dream of full-grown white ibis birds in Coral Gables, Miami, pausing for a moment to feed within the lush, green palms and tropical hibiscus blooms. They take flight, gracefully swooping in arcs with the warm, salty sea breeze against the backdrop of new developments. *This is like collaborative writing*, my dream conscious pronounces. *But how?* I ask. *How is this like collaborative writing?* Silence ensues before the dream channel suddenly changes. Smaller northern birds—black shadows on the grey sky—fight the wind, circling vast stretches of post-industrial riverfront. The dream lens has not changed from color to black and white. The color filter remains on; it is simply that the colors all pull from the greyscale palette. *Is this (un)collaborative writing?* I ask. I am only greeted with more silence.

8:29 a.m.

The wind and songbirds have calmed, and I awaken again to continue writing, to continue (un)collaboratively writing a dream. I hope my dream conscious lingers long-enough to remember.

8:48 a.m.

One still writes alone. Nobody writes and everybody writes.

7:32 a.m., six days later.

I am awakened by a nautical vessel in the international channel as it enters one prolonged blast. The sound signal indicates an obstruction in the waterway. I cannot recall what I dreamed. I hope it was not about collaborative writing.

Out the window, the songbirds sweep across the last of the fall winds. The river-birds follow suit. In the distance, against the metallic glimmer of a down-town skyscraper in the early morning light, they almost look like ibises.

An Almost Collaborative "Mo(ve)ment"

We performed this (un)collaborative writing in an impromptu reading of theory, images, and the spoken word. Two writers holding one virtually printed copy, passing it back and forth. Because, in thinking two and writing one, one writer had printed the second-to-last version. One writer had printed the past. A past of many (un)collaborative writings ago—one that differs from this collaborative writing in this now-frozen present, and one that will differ from future (un)col-laborative writings to come. An (un)collaborative writing mo(ve)ment (Davies & Gannon, 2006) already undone.

AND

Epistemic and ontological proliferation and movement toward post-qualitative research calls for different forms and conceptualizations of writing that are respon-sive to diverse ways of knowing and practicing critical social science (e.g., Lather & St. Pierre, 2013; St. Pierre, 2011). We follow calls to expand scholarly writing (e.g., Bridges-Rhoads & Van Cleave, 2014; Richardson, 2000; Richardson & St. Pierre, 2005) to make it more (in)accessible and (un)responsive to research processes and shifting ontological positionings. Calling and labeling a process collaborative writ-ing does not make it collaborative or even writing. Maybe nothing or everything does. If one does not continue from where another one cannot end, how can one write collaboratively? How can one write collaboratively in the absence of indi-vidual self and negotiated authorship? Is collaborative writing (un)desirable, (im)possible, (un)ethical? Or is it so dearly and sweetly oxymoronic that one cannot live without the other?

Despite the crises of representation, diverse ontological turns, posts-, and anti-humanisms, collaborative writing (not) continuously produces in its unknown, thus challenging scholars and readers to face the unknown and uncertainty. It is a collaborative writing that cannot be taught, replicated, or generalized. It produces, erases, connects, explores, and disappears in unexpected ways. As these authors learn to swim, collaborative writing is like the impermanence of writing on the seashore. Virginia Woolf writes in *The Waves* (1931):

> As they neared the shore each bar rose, heaped itself, broke and swept a thin veil of white water across the sand. The wave paused, and then drew out again, sighing like a sleeper whose breath comes and goes unconsciously.

(p. 7)

Like writing that is traced in the sand moments before the waves begin crashing over the writing, we glide over the writing, wash the writing back out to sea as we swim, erasing it all. Erasing you, erasing me, erasing us. Erasing this collaborative writing-not.

No, this is not a collaborative writing.
Yes, this is a collaborative writing-not.
Maybe.

The waves broke on the shore.

(Woolf, 1931, p. 297, emphasis in original)

References

Barad, K. (2007). *Meeting the universe halfway: Quantum physics and the entanglement of matter and meaning.* Durham, NC: Duke University Press.

Barthes, R. (1977). *Image—music—text.* New York: Farrar, Straus and Giroux.

Barthes, R. (2012). *Writing degree zero* (A. Lavers & C. Smith, Trans.). New York: Hill and Wang.

Brkich, C. A., & Barko, T. (2012). "Our most lethal enemy?" Star Trek, the Borg, and methodological simplicity. *Qualitative Inquiry, 18*(9), 787–797.

Bourassa, A. (2002) Literature, language, and the non-human. In B. Massumi (Ed.), *A shock to thought: Expression after Deleuze and Guattari* (pp. 60–76). London: Routledge.

Bridges-Rhoads, S. (2015). Writing paralysis in (post) qualitative research. *Qualitative Inquiry, 21*(8), 704–710.

Bridges-Rhoads, S., & Van Cleave, J. (2014). Pursuing responsibility: Writing and citing subjects in qualitative research. *Qualitative Inquiry, 20*(5), 641–652.

Davies, B., & Gannon, S. (2006). *Doing collective biography: Investigating the production of subjectivity.* Berkshire, UK: Open University Press.

Deleuze, G. (1994). *The logic of sense* (P. Patton, Trans.). New York: Columbia University Press. (Original work published 1968).

Deleuze, G. (1995). *Negotiations, 1972–1990* (M. Joughin, Trans.). New York: Columbia University Press. (Original work published 1990).

Deleuze, G., & Guattari, Felix. (1987). *A thousand plateaus: Capitalism and schizophrenia* (B. Massumi, Trans). Minneapolis: University of Minnesota Press. (Original work published 1980).

Derrida, J. (1976). *Of grammatology* (G. Spivak, Trans.). Baltimore, MD: The Johns Hopkins University Press. (Original work published 1967).

Derrida, J. (1987). *The post card: From Socrates to Freud and beyond* (A. Bass, Trans.). Chicago: The University of Chicago Press. (Original work published 1980).

Derrida, J., & Weber, E. (1995). *Points: Interviews, 1974–1994.* Stanford, CA: Stanford University Press.

Foucault, M. (1998). This is not a pipe (R. Hurley, Trans.). In J. Faubion (Ed.), *Aesthetics, method, and epistemology* (pp. 187–203). New York: The New Press.

Gale, K., & Wyatt, J. (2009). *Between the two: A nomadic inquiry into collaborative writing and subjectivity.* Newcastle upon Tyne, UK: Cambridge Scholars Publishing.

Guttorm, H. E., Hilton, K. A., Jonsdottir, G. U., Löytönen, T., McKenzie, L., Gale, K., & Wyatt, J. (2013). Encountering Deleuze. *International Review of Qualitative Research, 5*(4), 377–398.

Hannula, M., Suoranta, J., & Vaden, T. (2014). *Artistic research methodology*. New York: Peter Lang.

Hendricks, J. (2015). *Experimental and productive video: Connections and sensations in a Deleuzian ontological frame.* Presentation at the Eleventh International Congress of Qualitative Inquiry, Urbana-Champaign, IL.

Hofsess, B. A., & Sonenberg, J. L. (2013). Enter ho/rhizoanalysis. *Cultural Studies↔Critical Methodologies, 13*(4), 299–308.

Jackson, A., & Mazzei, L. (2012). *Thinking with theory in qualitative research: Viewing data across multiple perspectives.* London: Routledge.

Keane, J. (2015) Eight very vary(s): Towards a program of mistakes-on-purpose. *Inflexions, 8*, 95–109.

Koro-Ljungberg, M. (2015). Untitled photographs. Scottsdale, AZ.

Koro-Ljungberg, M. (2016). *Reconceptualizing qualitative research: Methodologies without methodology.* Thousand Oaks, CA: Sage Publications.

Koro-Ljungberg, M., Hendricks, J., & Ulmer, J. (2014). *Repetitions* [Film]. Presentation at the 10th International Congress of Qualitative Inquiry, Urbana-Champaign, IL.

Koro-Ljungberg, M., & Ulmer, J. (2015). Vital illusions, images, and education. In G. Canella, M. Pérez, & P. Pasque (Eds.), *Critical qualitative inquiry: Foundations and futures* (pp. 215–242). Walnut Creek, CA: Left Coast Press.

Lather, P., & St. Pierre, E. A. (2013). Post-qualitative research. *International Journal of Qualitative Studies in Education, 26*(6), 629–633.

Löytönen, T., Koro-Ljungberg, M., Carlson, D., Orange, A., & Cruz, J. (2015). A pink writing experiment. *Reconceptualizing Educational Research Methodology, 6*(1), 23–39.

Malabou, C. (2010). *Plasticity at the dusk of writing: Dialectic, destruction, deconstruction.* New York: Columbia University Press.

Massumi, B. (2002). *Parables for the virtual.* Durham, NC: Duke University Press.

Pederson, R. (2006, May 3). This is not a pipe (the title is a ripoff from Michael Foucault) [Photograph]. Creative Commons CC BY-SA 2.0 license. Retrieved from https://www.flickr.com/photos/chefranden/139936174/in/photolist-dnd9E-6nJmDa-aqRMJe-dsyPNZ-db8Ac3-4FRmzv-5RHRu3-8vFGYH-pQWeJH-6AfVnt-avn2rq-dMMQet-rL8XQs-5oRDoM-4aRLHB-q6t8Kv-eeVimw-bTjjax-bEpzo9-bTjhWB-bEpy9S-bEpxro-bEpwAQ-bTjfba-9QwUzq-5KkoUW-j6MpJK-cy9ABs-7zFWiL-7zFNP7-6GSN8F-7zFPvu-7zC44g-bEpvsU-5LfgPF-j48GQ-7zC542-7zCbKe-7zCbw2-7zCbiK-7zCaSx-7zCaGn-7zFVGw-7zFVtE-7zFVdN-7zFUXW-7zC4xX-7zFP1J-7zFN5q-7zC2Bn.

Richardson, L. (2000). New writing practices in qualitative research. *Sociology of Sport Journal, 17*(1), 5–20.

Richardson, L., & St. Pierre, E. (2005). Writing: A method of inquiry. In N. Denzin & Y. Lincoln (Eds.), *The Sage handbook of qualitative research* (3rd ed., pp. 959–978). Thousand Oaks: Sage.

Sableman, P. (2010, September 15). Borderland construction 1921—Tuscon, Arizona [Photograph]. Creative Commons CC BY 2.0 license. Retrieved from https://www.flickr.com/photos/pasa/4997447793/.

Sputzer, S. (2011, September 18). Sand [Photograph]. Creative Commons CC BY 2.0 license. Retrieved from https://www.flickr.com/photos/10413717@N08/6215717388/.

St. John, J. (2013, March 14). Mudcracks along the shoreline of Storr's Lake (San Salvador Island, Bahamas) 4 [Photograph]. Creative Commons CC-BY 2.0 license. Retrieved from https://www.flickr.com/photos/jsjgeology/16708794926/in/photolist-rsuWB9-4twAtG-nqnSVz-qxN94j-4CRbjP-4CR9KX-c8LUrW-7NTnfv-7NTnkX-iBBmZV-7NXca7-7NXceJ-94NYnC-in9xEZ-beHyNa-cDj2tE-cYjLE7-cDYtp7-9z

CY3n-e48Yd9–7NXbS1-apQNZL-7rcQuE-8sEwWD-94KW2V-8yPZSW-dcGv
m2-nHZx7J-bdrrqa-7S3d7n-fEknyM-ohRdd5-fwSFhh-bPNM3D-9PHx
1h-2yAqC6-ioANX-afxBte-oZKyPU-phfv1c-oZLhWB-pfdu63-oZKywQ-bw
S4Ec-9NHxHV-bufoVj-dQBbTU-ck2Tmw-pJooj2–8nfF5X.

St. Pierre, E. A. (2011). Post qualitative research: The critique and the coming after. In N. K. Denzin & Y. S. Lincoln (Eds.), *The Sage handbook of qualitative research* (4th ed., pp. 611–626). Thousand Oaks, CA: Sage Publications.

Ulmer, J. (2015). Embodied writing: Choreographic composition as methodology. *Research in Dance Education, 16*(1), 33–50.

Ulmer, J., & Koro-Ljungberg, M. (2015). Writing visually through (methodological) events and cartography. *Qualitative Inquiry, 21*(2), 138–152.

Van Cleave, J., & Bridges-Rhoads, S. (2013). "As cited in" writing partnerships: The (im) possibility of authorship in postmodern research. *Qualitative Inquiry, 19*(9), 674–685.

Woolf, V. (1931). *The waves.* New York: Harcourt Brace.

Wyatt, J., Gale, K., Gannon, S., & Davies, B. (2010). Deleuzian thought and collaborative writing: A play in four acts. *Qualitative Inquiry, 16*(9), 730–741.

Wyatt, J., Gale, K., Gannon, S., & Davies, B. (2011). *Deleuze & collaborative writing: An immanent plane of composition.* New York: Peter Lang.

SECTION III
Performing Inquiry

8

WRITTEN RAW

Omissions, Overshares, and the Shameful Ethics of Personal Narrative

Sophie Tamas

Dear Publisher,

I would like to offer my latest book for your consideration. *Intimate Studies* is the non-fiction account of a formerly religious, feminist academic small-town mom who recruits a young lover to fill the gap she created by kicking out a partner with posttraumatic stress disorder. She spends the next eight months writing her way through her peculiar past and present, trying to make sense of the mess that sex, gender, and power have made in her life. The resulting memoir takes readers from the Arctic to Africa, through secrets and trauma, into the heart of how and why we love, and how we let go. While the tale is compelling on its own, the author's ability to tell it draws on nine years of doctoral and post-doctoral research on domestic abuse, memory, and representation, to provide a smart, self-aware, somewhat neurotic third-person narrator who questions herself and her own story.

Without hiding in theory, she tackles the moral, ethical, and practical complexity of living and writing about intimate relationships—not just with romantic partners, but also with children, parents, colleagues, and friends. The story takes a hard look at tough issues—including incest, faith, adultery, and mental illness—without allowing them to displace the everyday and beautiful. It doesn't provide a facile happy ending but leaves readers with the more durable hope that comes from recognition, acceptance, and the generosity of opening toward one another.

Now imagine that your daughter has written this book. Would you want to read it? Would you wish that she had waited till you're dead?

If you had written it, would you show your mother? If another relative that you've written about, that you love, worked in your field and didn't know about the book, would you do a conference paper on it and let that paper be published?

If the president of Random House Canada said the writing was sensational, would that make it okay?

The book is a still point in the centre of a tornado. At the centre of the still point, there is a naked nine-year-old girl, lying on her back. At the centre of the girl, a pinprick opening into a black hole of shame.

This chapter is a collection of fragments plucked from the tornado.

1. Last year at the International Congress of Qualitative Inquiry, over pints at a pub, I asked several autoethnographers what they would do if their ex said, "I don't want you to write about me."

"Your stories are yours," they said. "You have to write what you can live with."

How do you know what you can live with? And what does that tell you?

2. I gave my mother a copy of the book. "If my daughter had written it, I'd want to know," I said. I meant, but did not say, I'd want to know *her*. Sure you do, now, my mother could have said. Get back to me when she's 43.

It has been difficult. I don't know how to talk about that difficulty without making my mother feel even more over-exposed, or misdirecting your sympathies. She has, several times, stopped reading the book and said she can't read any more. After several conversations I've said that I can't discuss it with her more until she's read it. So we are at an impasse.

Writing—even something as small as this paper—could end the impasse, one way or another, so I'm afraid. Our relationship has had the wind knocked out of it; it is lying between us, flat on its back. She is afraid that if she speaks to me she will be quoted. I am afraid that I can't think without writing, and can't write across this space without quoting her.

Meanwhile, we set signal fires of love, hoping each other will spot them. She brings me sausages and pork hocks from her favourite butcher in the city. I give her trays of morning glories and sweet peas and nasturtiums that I have grown from seed in my one good south-facing window.

It is not enough, but life goes on.

3. We each see different sides of what this book might do. My mother's list of possibilities includes divorce, suicide, estrangement, and being unable to look people in the eye. She feels like she is being judged with no opportunity for defence. She asks if there are ethical standards in my field. I say most authors seem to manage by not writing about their family until their parents are dead.

"That would have been good," she says. Good for whom?

"No," I say. "That means giving up on the possibility of growth and change."

She can accept that I needed to write it, but she doesn't see any potential benefit to publishing it.

"Haven't you ever read someone's story, about hard shit they went through, and felt grateful that they shared their experiences?" I ask.

She says no. No. Even 'sharing circles' are unfair because people can be falsely accused.

I am trying to hear her, without being defensive.

4. I am feeling defensive. The book is not about her; she rarely appears on the page. When she does, I call her "the headwaters of my own humanity" and admit that I have let my fear of judgement matter more to me than her loneliness. I frame this recognition as a productive use of shame. Readers who don't know her have said she comes across on the page as sweet and loving. The relational patterns I describe in the book fit a well-documented template for a particular kind of family; we're nothing new. My mother's response is predictable. She could be reading from a script.

It is so easy to reduce mothers to caricatures.

5. What I think this book might do.

I have been working with a mentor, through a book development program at the Banff Centre. He says it is valuable and beautifully written. There is no way to avoid collateral damage. The reader won't think of anyone as villainous or predatory. I've taken on the least-publicized issue out there, an elephant in many rooms. He asks, "Who is going to come forward?"

Every now and then someone reads my other book, on the aftermath of domestic abuse, and writes to thank me for being so open (Tamas, 2011). They feel validated, recognized, more free to speak about their own experiences. They say my writing helps. I am struck by their kindness, pleased to have made some use of loss. And I hear Nietzsche's (1968) warning: "[P]erhaps there has never before been a more dangerous ideology ... than this will to good" (p. 192–193).

I told my mother I wrote the book to push relational patterns to the surface, to interrupt intergenerational transmission, so they would not shape my daughter's lives. Let them make new mistakes. But writing the book was also a heart bypass machine, built on the ability and need to dissociate and observe while I was emotionally hemorrhaging. It was reclaiming and naming secrets that others could hold over me. It aspires to self-acceptance, to solidarity with the broken, crazy people that we study from a distance as if we've been there but are over it, looking back and down on what we used to be.

Maybe it was a form of recreational masochism, written as an extreme sport that offers the rush of a brush with disaster. Or perhaps it's just a symptom. I could be driven by posttraumatic repetition compulsion to self-wound, to test the sharpened edge of my control, to see how far I can go. The ultra-marathon junkie who runs until his toenails fall off is not cast in the same light as the cutter, on the shameful end of the hierarchy of pain.

Remember: It's just a book.

6. Avery Gordon (2008) describes haunting as a potentially generative process in which an unrecognized injustice troubles us and will not rest and pushes us toward something to be done. It might cost you your life and may be hopeless, but in myths and movies and fairy tales the hero does something to change the situation.

In between our various difficult conversations, my mother gave me a medicine bundle: a solid lump, the size and shape of a ciabatta bun, wrapped in a red scrap of fabric. She held it out in both hands, explaining its origins and insufficiency. She wanted to give me something, to recognize my suffering, but knew this wasn't enough. Eventually, I stepped in to stem the tide of apology with a hug. Under her winter coat her bones felt small as a songbird's. We both took a breath.

I received the bundle in order to give us both something-to-be-done. So the bereaved, if they are gracious and kind, accept casseroles and pies from their neighbours. Later, I started unwrapping the cloth, to investigate the contents of the leather pouch inside, but I stopped. The more I looked, the less there'd be. I was missing the point.

When my mother appeals to privacy, perhaps she is saying that her family life, the relational interior, loses its identity and power if it is unwrapped, its contents itemized on the bed. But for me the book itself is just another bundle, with me and my people like so many inscrutable things, wrapped up inside and given away, with two hands. "To be able to share," says Linda Tuhiwai Smith, "to have something worth sharing, gives dignity to the giver" (1999, p. 105). By offering my stories, drawing readers in to see the things that scare and shame and delight me, I gain dignity. One reader wrote to me after ordering my first book. "I have it in my bag," she said. "I haven't opened it yet. It feels like I'm carrying a Christmas present."

7. If writing is the casserole I bring myself, my something-to-be-done, it could still be dangerous. The need to do something, to fix and feel effective, propels all sorts of poor choices. Margaret Price (2011) calls it a "whitely response to making a mistake" that echoes with the desire to annihilate whatever appears to be broken (p. 18). Anything can feel better than doing nothing, and bad outcomes are easily written-off by good intent. Something-to-be-done can be a coping mechanism, a margin of busyness around unbearable circumstances, that blunts the edge of our discomfort so it never becomes acute enough to push us across a frightening threshold of change.

There is a danger in mistaking something-to-be-done for a solution, a hero quest that saves the day. These acts are an end in themselves, rituals that require no external outcome, driven by need rather than reason. I will be disappointed and embarrassed if I expect to be all better when I'm done. I might go on indefinitely, thinking I'm not done because I'm still not better. Writing is not exorcism, and feelings are not problems to be solved. They need to be witnessed. That's why therapists listen, and teach us containment, to tolerate the discomfort of bearing witness to ourselves.

In dominant linear Western ways of thinking, sight equals progress equals knowledge and buried things acquire value once they're unearthed. The absent and unseen are framed in terms of erasure, loss, and repression. But I recently attended a heritage conservation workshop where one of the participants sipped her plastic cup of wine and talked about fallow time, when places are inaccessible or hidden, gathering value that will be released in the future. Another participant described archaeologists who, lacking the means to preserve and display their finds, document and bury things back where they found them.

This reminds me of Clarissa Pinkola Estes (1999), talking about the necessity and value of dark times, and of Ernesto Javier Martínez's (2008) notion of *joto passivity*, a practice of deliberate quietude that is not the same as doing nothing. Fallow time cannot be rushed. You sit. You trust. You wait. It takes patience and maturity. I may be too whitely to listen, to let my stories rest in the dark, unexplained. To draw meaning from them gradually, unprocessed, the way the earth draws nutrients from wind-fallen fruit, without thinking it's a waste.

8. Primo Levi says "a book has to be a telephone that works" (cited in Probyn, 2005, p. 157). In order for the gesture of writing to be complete, I need someone to pick up the receiver. Otherwise it is a casserole, meant for the bereaved, spoiling on my counter. What the recipient thinks of it seems mostly irrelevant. My mother is right: They might think that it—that I, that we—are disgusting. That would feel terrible. But would that make it wrong to publish? If we based our ethics on aversion to what hurts, none of us would ever have been born.

Melissa Orlie (1997) argues that living ethically means thinking and acting in collaboration with others, in order to recognize and forgive our inevitable trespasses and work "toward mutual transfiguration" (p. 174). Responsiveness, opening ourselves to others with a willingness to change and reveal who we are becoming, is a major element of political action. The selves we bring to that exchange borrow a sense of cohesion and reliability from the way we are recognized and received by others. We don't really exist as stable units of one. This means rethinking boundaries; the public that my mum would keep out-there is already inside our secrets, telling us what they mean.

My mother understands shame as a guardian of social order, deterring us from wrong, but our cop-in-the-head is often cruel. Following Elspeth Probyn (2005), I see shame as a bodily response to broken connection or interest. The object of that interest could be anything; what triggers shame will vary, but the list is generally shorter for white, straight, healthy, wealthy men. Your body will react. You can trust it to react. But you cannot trust the meaning you ascribe to that reaction.

Every time I say "this happened to me," someone says "me too." Publishing under a pen-name could shield my family but would leave these people disavowed. Because I am protected by privilege, even though it's scary and awkward I feel some responsibility to speak up, to share ways of thinking about and outlasting everyday unbearable things, beyond useless hurtful hard binaries of right and wrong, public and private, dirty and pure.

9. "Either ethics makes no sense at all," says Deleuze (1990/1969), "or this is what it means and has nothing else to say: not to be unworthy of what happens to us" (p. 148–9). What does it mean, to be worthy?

I fold a constellation of relationships and events into the page, and connect the dots outward, into a larger space that Berlant (2011) calls an "intimate public," built around personal stories "about not being defeated by what is overwhelming" (p. 227). Or being defeated, being unworthy, and writing anyway, because it's all that I can do, even in the eye of a tornado.

10. "I'm sorry I never got a chance to be the good, pure girl you wanted me to be," I said to my mother. I was zipping up my coat, crying in our small-town hipster cafe, because I've made her so sad.

"I have never seen any badness in you," she said, "not even one speck."

I am holding that thought against the places I have written raw.

References

Berlant, L. (2011). *Cruel optimism*. Durham, NC: Duke University Press.

Deleuze, G. (1990/1969). *The logic of sense*. Ed. C.V. Boundas. Trans. M. Lester. New York: Columbia University Press.

Gordon, A. (2008). *Ghostly matters: Haunting and the sociological imagination*. Minneapolis: University of Minnesota Press.

Martínez, Ernesto Javier. (2008). Reflections on joto passivity. *Future of Minority Studies National Conference*. Atlanta, GA: Spelman College.

Nietzsche, F. (1968). *The will to power*. Ed. W. Kauffmann. Trans. W. Kauffmann & R.J. Hollingdale. New York: Vintage.

Orlie, M. (1997). *Living ethically, acting politically*. Ithaca, NY: Cornell University Press.

Pinkola Estes, C. (1999). The story of la calavera. In *Theatre of the imagination (volume 1)*. Louisville, CO: Sounds True.

Price, M. (2011). Cripping revolution: A crazed essay. *Society for Disability Studies*. San Jose, CA, 18 June 2011. <https://margaretprice.wordpress.com/? attachment_id=183>.

Probyn, E. (2005). *Blush: Faces of shame*. Minneapolis: University of Minnesota Press.

Tamas, S. (2011). *Life after leaving: The remains of spousal abuse*. Walnut Creek, CA: Left Coast Press.

Tuhiwai Smith, L. (1999). *Decolonizing methodologies*. London: Zed Books.

9

WRITING IN/THROUGH THE IN BETWEEN

Messy Middles and Cartoon Clouds

Patricia Leavy

I recently revised my first novel, Low-Fat Love, *to release an anniversary edition. The process made me feel surprisingly nostalgic and reflective. In this autoethnographic piece I dig into my past to explore the implicit and personal motivations for originally writing the novel.*

I've come to learn that when we talk about our research there is what is true and there is what is more true.

Here are some true stories.

People ask me why I took 10 years of impressions from interviews and wrote my first novel, *Low-Fat Love.* Why fiction?

I give them my speech. "Well, over the years I cumulatively learned from my interviews with women as well as teaching experiences and I had nowhere to share the overarching insights I had gleaned or to offer unapologetic advice. I needed the freedom to get my ideas out. Blah, blah, blah."

Without fail a hand goes up.

"What is low-fat love exactly?" she asks.

"Lite love. Lite. L. I. T. E. Think butter substitute. I *can* believe it's not butter. Low-fat love is like that, but in our relationships, in *ourselves.*"

Smiles. Resonance.

But I wonder to myself: Where's the space for what's more true? Why did I start collecting interviews with women in the first place? Why did I hear my students' personal stories as tales of the to-be-named concept of low-fat love? Why did I seek this out? How did I shape what I saw?

Full stop. Cycle back.

Before I started writing *Low-Fat Love* I scribbled this line on a piece of note-book paper:

She exists in the middle.

I'd like to share a secret with you. I'm obsessed with the middle. It's where I've always lived.

Here's a memory:

When I was in elementary school I was bullied daily. I was truly tormented. Shy, quiet, and awkward, I retreated into myself when they screamed things like, "You're so fucking ugly you should die."

Writing was my refuge. I could always build a story-world to crawl into and hide in plain sight, right in the middle of madness.

Flash forward to another memory:

Graduate school. In a bathroom stall, the ladies room. I'm pregnant with my daughter and going through a hard time adjusting to this unexpected state of expectedness. Two women come into the bathroom chatting away. The feminist-in-name-only professor who made me cry earlier that week when she criticized me for getting pregnant and insinuated I was suddenly a lost cause was with a grad student in my cohort who fancies herself the polar opposite of me. I wear makeup and high heels and brush the long hair from my eyes. I'm not serious. I'm a joke to her. She doesn't utter a word in a sentence that anyone without a PhD could understand. She likes to make sure we all know how smart she is. You know, big-word smart.

Pause. Flashback footnote.

I'm in my elementary school guidance office with my parents. I'm scared having them in school with me. What if someone screams, "Die ugly girl"? I don't want them to hear that. Luckily that doesn't happen. Relief. Instead they're told that I'm not very smart and they "shouldn't expect much from me."

I don't say a word but I think we all feel sad to learn that I'm stupid.

Pause over. Back to the bathroom stall in graduate school.

So-called feminist professor says: "She'll never finish now. And I've invested so much time in her."

Graduate student responds: "Have you met her boyfriend? He's such Eurotrash."

They continue on, do their business, and leave; all the while I hideout in the stall.

I wanted to correct them. David, my partner at the time, was born and raised in Africa, where he lived until after college. I guess one accent was the same as another to them. The grad student debates the nuanced meaning of six-syllable words in footnotes, but all accents are homogenized. I wanted to find her to correct her error, but I never said a word. Not about any of it.

As a footnote, David, my daughter's father, died in 2014 after a six-year battle with lung cancer. We had broken up years earlier, and, as Laurel Richardson told me, there's no card for the ex. It's an in-between space. But no less grief filled.

Flash to 2013.

Double book release, keynotes, media interviews. People are smiling at me but I wonder if they think I can't hear. It's not their fault. Sometimes I pretend I can't. Here are a couple comments I pretend not to hear before delivering an international keynote address:

"She's too hot to be smart."

"I read her books. I didn't think she'd be young or pretty."

"She's so fem, but she must be sharp."

I take the stage. In my mind I am thinking: How is it that in one lifetime I could be too ugly to live, and too pretty to think?

Pause. Flashback.

Pediatrician's office, age 10. Annual eye exam. I look in the viewfinder and say what direction each letter E is facing. The nurse asks:

"Well, you got them all perfectly right, but can you tell me why you read them backwards?"

I sit silently. I don't know what she's talking about.

She says:

"You read it from right to left, not left to right."

I am silent. My mother makes a joke. We leave.

Update.

It would be years before I would learn that I am dyslexic. My thoughts were somewhere in between; this is good news because maybe I'm not stupid, and this is horrible news because maybe it confirms that little should be expected of me.

Flash forward to 2014. I'm on the telephone with my publisher going over her notes on my latest book manuscript. She's talking about something in chapter 2, but I can't find it. I ask her to please tell me the page number and how many lines down. She does and we proceed on. At the end of the conversation she says something about being sorry if she was hard to follow but she's really busy. Now is my chance. It has taken me more than a dozen books to lose my fear of being perceived of as stupid so I say, "It's no problem. It's just that I have dyslexia and I can't find something on a page quickly without more direction."

Silence. She tells me she is flabbergasted. She seems equally surprised that I have published so much and that this had never come up before. I tell her that if she saw my process she'd be surprised she ever got any content from me. I am a sloooow reader. I have to be. But the writing comes quickly.

Just to clarify, I'm not stupid. I just read slowly.

The present:

My daughter: Madeline is a freshman in high school. There is nothing she loves more than reading and writing. She dreams of becoming an author. She recently applied to a competitive summer creative writing program and asked me to proofread her admissions essay.

Paralleling my own childhood experiences, Madeline was horribly bullied for years in elementary school. I wish we didn't have this in common. She was tormented so badly that we moved. In her admissions essay she wrote, "Reading and writing have always been my alternative to therapy."

I think to myself, "Yeah, I get that."

These days people frequently ask me about writing. They want to know about my process and any tips I can offer. But my daughter is the only person who has ever asked me this: "What does it *feel like* when you're writing?"

My answer to her: "It feels like the clouds in the sky are cartoon clouds and suddenly there's a big silver zipper across those cartoon clouds. I unzip it and crawl in. No one sees me. I'm in the middle of a cartoon cloud and I write and I write and eventually I write my way out, back into plain sight. Does that make sense or do I sound crazy?"

Madeline smiles. "I totally get that. It's how I feel when I write or read." We hug.

So, what was the point of all of this?

I live in the between. In between hideous and beautiful. In between stupid and smart. In between fiction and nonfiction. The middle is my space. It's my productive space.

What's true and what's more true?

Sometimes the gap between true and more true, or truer, is the gap between what we say versus what we are thinking. And therein is the possibility of fiction. *Interiority.* Interior monologue. What people are *thinking and feeling.*

What's true and what's more true?

How did my novel *Low-Fat Love* come to be?

Every project has a seed.

I live in the middle. Being in the middle, the productive and painful in-betweens, draws me to in-between*ness.* I search for it in others. Searching for my people through their stories. Building empathetic bridges.

So, when people ask me why I took 10 years of research and wrote *Low-Fat Love,* I say, "Well, over the years I cumulatively learned from my interviews with women as well as teaching experiences and I had nowhere to share the overarching insights I had gleaned or to offer unapologetic advice. I needed the freedom to get my ideas out. Blah, blah, blah."

That is true, but here is what is more true. The day I secretly started writing *Low-Fat Love* I found the piece of paper that said, "She exists in the middle." It was the seed and I planted it.

My daughter is also the only person to ask me if I have any favorite lines in *Low-Fat Love*.

My answer: "Yes." My favorite lines are:

> "Prilly lived in between who she was and who she wanted to be. Prilly was in the middle."

10

FRAGMENTS OF A WESTERN SELF[1]

Norman K. Denzin

Coda Number One

Justice Now: A One-Act Play

"Fragments of a Western Self," a one-act play, with 11 scenes, uses Bud Goodall's discourse to create a critical autoethnographic account of the author's histories with his family, the postmodern West, and Native Americans.

Characters: Bud Goodall, Sandra Goodall, Author, Grandmother, Guy Maddin, Tonto

Speaker One; Speaker Two

Staging Notes: Performers are seated around a seminar table on the third floor of Gregory Hall, a four-story, 125-year-old brick classroom on the campus of the University of Illinois. There are 25 chairs along the walls and around a 40-feet long wood table. Two large nature paintings on loan from the art department hang on the north and east walls of the room. There is a pull-down screen at the south end of the room for projecting video. Overhead lights are dimmed. Sun streams in through the two north windows. It is 1:00 in the afternoon. The time is the present. The text of the play is handed from speaker to speaker. The first speaker reads the text for Speaker One, the second speaker reads the text for Speaker Two, and so forth, to the end.

Curtain Rises

Off stage the Dave Brubeck quartet quietly plays "Take Five."

Speaker One: Bud Goodall

When I decided to make this website the "Jr." appendage to the body of my name just finally seemed extraneous. I am a man full grown. My father has been dead a long time, and there are no fixed rules in the U.S. for when a Jr. becomes a Sr. So I respectfully erased it. I liked the results. H. L. Goodall was again reborn. In America, as every writer knows, ours is a heritage of personal reinvention. I still don't know if I truly own my name. A good friend of mine, and fine fellow writer, keeps calling me Hal. I've gotten mail recently for Hud Goodall. My friendly barista down at the local Starbucks can't seem to remember "Bud" so I've taken to calling myself Cricket. Who knows what name I'll die with? My journey is not yet complete.

(Bud's Facebook page, 2012)

Lights dim, curtain comes down.

Coda Number Two

Curtain rises. Spotlight shines on solitary speaker, center stage. The Brubeck quartet continues to play.

Speaker One: Author as Narrator Number One

Before I started writing about my family, Indians, and the New West, I read everything Bud had written about writing the new ethnography (2000, 2008a, 2008b; see also Amira de la Garza, Krizek, & Trujillo, 2012). I got all tangled up with issues of autoethnography, creative nonfiction, the plural present, voice narrative arc, counter-narrative, point of view, reflexivity, and metaphor. But somewhere in Bud's writings I found the courage to experiment. I did not want to write a standard ethnography. I wanted to write from my experiences in the new West.[2] I wanted to critically challenge the version of the West as it had been presented to me as a child.

Speaker Two: Bud (Narrative Aside, to Audience)

I call it the postmodern West, a mythic genocidal frontier filled with an overlay of monuments, theme parks, casinos, dude ranches, and fake buffalo herds.

(2009, p. 30)

Speaker One: Author

I learned from Greg Ulmer that the biographical project begins with the sting of childhood memory, with an event that lingers and remains in the person's life story (Ulmer, 1989, p. 209). In writing a mystory the writer creates the conditions for rediscovering the meanings of these events from the past (Ulmer, 1989, p. 211). New ways of performing and experiencing the past are created.

To represent the past this way does not mean to "recognize it 'the way it really was.' It means to seize hold of a memory as it flashes up at a moment of danger" (Benjamin, 1969, p. 257). To see and re-discover the past not as a succession of events, but as a series of scenes, inventions, emotions, images, and stories.

(Ulmer, 1989, p. 112)

Scene One: The Author's German Ancestry

Off stage, a German band, the Johnny Ca$H Brothers, quietly plays cowboy music.

Speaker One: Narrator as Author

Remember these facts: German males like to play Indian. According to Der Indianer: 40,000 Germans spend their weekends dressed as Native Americans (Lopinto, 2009, p. 798). And that's not all. The Karl May Festival in Bad Segeberg, the largest of the annual German and Austrian Karl May Wild West festivals, attracts over 300,000 people a year to its open-air stage.

(Gruber, 2004)[3]

Speaker Two: Narrator as Family Historian

1920: My father, a twin, was born to German parents in Aberdeen, South Dakota. **1871**: My father's great grandfather, August Froelich, a cabinet maker, came to America from Brandenburg, Germany, settling first in Horicon, Wisconsin, and then moving to the Dakota Territory in **1888**.[4] This was two years before the Battle at Wounded Knee, and 12 years after Custer's Last Stand

(Denzin, 2011)

Scene Two: German Indians R US[5]

Speaker One: Narrator to Audience

1960–1975: My father disappeared from my life, moving first to Detroit and then to New Orleans, where he was employed by the Army Corps of Engineers as a captain on a barge working from New Orleans to Baton Rouge on the Mississippi River. When he came back into my life he called himself Captain Ken.

1984: My father, aka Captain Ken, moved from New Orleans to the Amana Colonies, a German settlement in central Iowa, twenty miles from the Fox (Mesquaki) Indian Reservation.

1988: My father and step-mother Leslie took a two-week tour sponsored by the Amana Societies to Germany, visiting eight German cities in 10 days, including Cologne, Dresden, Frankfurt, Hamburg, Leipzig, and Munich. They had tickets to the "Oberammergau Passion Play"[6] and the Karl May Festival, in Bad Segeberg, just north of Hamburg. They took a side-trip to Brandenberg, hoping to meet relatives of August Froelich. He came back with postcards of Germans dressed up as Indians playing Indian in the Karl May Festival.

Speaker Two: Author as Narrator Number One

My father was drawn to Indians, to watching Indians perform.

1950–1955: When we were young our little family made several visits to Tama, Iowa, to the Fox and Mesquaki Indian Reservation.

Speaker One: Narrator as Historian (Narrative Aside to Audience)

I'm going to assume that these Fox Indians were relatives of the Fox Indians who performed with George Catlin's Traveling Indian Gallery in London in 1840.

(See Denzin, 2013a)

Speaker Two: Narrator as Expert

This is correct.

Speaker One: Author as Narrator Number Two

Each time we visited the reservation we would buy Indian clothing, like moccasins and Indian headbands. In this way we learned how to dress like little Indians. Grandpa and Grandma Townsley brought us cowboy outfits, leather chaps, cowboy boots, cowboy hats, Indian bows and arrows, and Indian headbands.

Speaker Two: Author as Narrator Number One

Soon we would play at being Lone Ranger and Tonto, sometimes Red Rider and Little Beaver. We took turns being an Indian or a cowboy, except the Indian was always killed.

Speaker One: Author as Narrator Number Three

When I started this writing project in 1994 I was 53 years old. I had White guilt about all my performances as a pretend Indian. I was also angry about the treatment of Indians by the U.S. government, but I had no idea now to move forward beyond the guilt and the anger.

Scene Three: The Past: Docile

Indians

Speaker One: Narrator-as-Young-Boy

Let's start in the beginning. When I was little, in the 1940s, living in south central Iowa, my grandmother would tell stories about Indians. She loved to tell the story about the day a tall Indian brave with braided hair came to her mother's kitchen door and asked for some bread to eat. This happened when Grandma was a little girl, probably around 1915.

Speaker Two: Grandmother

This Indian was so polite and handsome. Grandma said his wife and children stood right behind him in a straight row. The Indian said his name was Mr. Thomas. He was a member of the Fox Indian Nation. He said that he and his wife and his children were traveling to the Mesquakie Reservation near Tama, Iowa, to visit relatives. Grandma said her mother believed him. He said that they had run out of money and did not like to ask for handouts, but this looked like a friendly farmhouse. Grandma said it is a crime in this country to be hungry! I believe that, too.

Speaker One (Why Wouldn't This Be Speaker Three? I Have to Admit That I Am Not Following the Speaker Nomenclature): Grandmother-as-Young-Daughter

Grandma's mother made lunch for Mr. Thomas and his family. They sat under the big oak tree in the front yard and had a picnic. Later, when they were leaving, Mr. Thomas came back to the kitchen and thanked Grandma's mother again. He gave her a small hand-woven wicker basket as a gift. I treasure to this day this basket. It has become a family heirloom.

Scene Four: Real Indians

Speaker One: Narrator-as-Young-Boy

June, 1955: On our last trip to the Tama Reservation, I remember wondering if we'd see Mr. Thomas, if I would even recognize him if he was there. We walked through the mud, past tepees to the center of a big field. Indians in ceremonial dress with paint on their faces and long braids of hair were singing and dancing. Some were drumming and singing. At the edge of the field, tables were set up under canvas tents. Dad bought some Indian fry bread for all of us, and bottles of cold root beer. We took the fry bread and pop back to the dance area and watched the dancers. Then it rained and the dancing stopped, and we got in the car and drove home.

Scene Five: Reel Indians

Speaker One: Narrator-as-Young-Boy

The next time I saw an Indian was a week after the Tama trip. Grandpa took me to a movie at the Strand Theater in Iowa City. We watched *Broken Arrow* with Jay Silverheels, Jimmy Stewart, Debra Paget, Will Geer, and Jeff Chandler, who played Chief Cochise. Those Indians did not look like the Indians on the

Tama Reservation. The Tama Indians were less real. They kind of looked like everybody else, except for the dancers in their ceremonial dress.

Scene Six: The Sting of Memory

Voice Two: Author (Narrative Aside, to Audience)

By revisiting my past through these remembered experiences, I insert myself in my family's history with Native Americans. This history is part of a deeper set of mid-century memories about Indians, reservations, life on the Midwest plains, and American culture. As I narrate these experiences, I begin to understand that I, along with my family, am a participant in this discourse. I am a player in a larger drama performing the parts culture gives to young white males. From the vantage of the present I can look back with a critical eye on those family performances, but the fact of my participation remains. We turned Native Americans into exotic cultural objects. We helped them perform non-threatening versions of Indian-ness, versions that conformed to those Indians I watched on the silver screen.

Voice One: Author (Second Narrative Aside to Audience)

Here is another string of childhood and young adulthood memories.

★★Saturday morning in my grandparents' living room. My brother and I are watching *The Lone Ranger*. I'm dressed up like Tonto, with a feather in a headband and a toy pistol in a fake leather holster strapped around my waist.

★★Thanksgiving, fourth grade, Coralville, Iowa: I'm dressed up as Squanto in the Thanksgiving play. My face is painted brown. My grandparents are in the audience.

★★Winter 1957: The Red Scare is everywhere. Father joins a Civilian Civil Defense Team, looking for low-flying Russian bombers.

★★People build bomb shelters.

★★Summer 1979: I'm older now, drinking and driving fast down country roads, playing loud country music. I'm a cowboy, not an Indian. My favorite singer and song is Willie Nelson's "Mama Don't Let Your Babies Grow Up to Be Cowboys."

★★Wedding, Winter 1963: I close my eyes and remember Sunday fish fries along the Iowa River, hayrides and football on Friday night, homecoming dances in the University High School gym, pretty girls in blue sweaters and white bobby socks, tall young men with blue suede shoes, flat-top haircuts, Elvis singing "Heart Break Hotel."

Speaker Two: Author (to Self)

I wish I could reach back and hold on to all of these things I loved then. James Lee Burke (2009) reminds me that the secret is "to hold on to the things you loved, and never give them up for any reason" (p. 274).[7] But did I really love them or was I just afraid to act like I didn't love them?

Speaker One: Author (to Audience)

Which self was I performing? Have I really talked myself into giving them up? I've always been performing, even in front of the black-and-white TV. For me the dividing line between person and character, performer and actor, stage and setting, script and text, performance and reality disappeared, if it ever existed. For a moment I was Tonto, and then I was Squanto, then the Lone Ranger, then Red Rider, then Little Beaver, white/red/cowboy/Indian. Illusion and make-believe prevail, we are who we are through our performative acts. Nothing more, nothing less.

Scene Seven: The Sting of Memory, One More Time

Voice One: Narrator

We became an A.A. family in 1957. The drinking had gone too far. Father announced that he was joining A.A. Soon my brother and I were going to Alateen meetings and mother joined Alanon. About one year later, Mom and Dad had some A.A. friends out for a cookout on the farm. There was a new couple, Shirley and George. Shirley had black hair like mom, and she was small and petite. She was wearing an orange dress that flowed all around her knees. Dad set up the archery set behind the lilacs in the side-yard. The men gathered with bows, and you could hear the twang of the arrows all the way back in the house. But nobody was very good.

★★★

Mom had Pete Fountain and his clarinet playing on the portable record player. Everybody came back in the house, and before you knew it the dining room was filled with dancing couples. Men and women in 1950s dress-up clothes, wide-collar shirts, pleated slacks, and greased-back hair. Women with Mamie Eisenhower bangs, hose, garter belts, and high heels. All of sudden Dad was dancing with Shirley, and Mom was in the kitchen fixing snacks. I thought Dad and Shirley were dancing a little close to just be friends.

★★★

About a month later our little world changed forever. I came home from high school and found a note from Dad. It was short and read, "I have to leave you. You and Mark are on your own now." I was 18 and Mark was 14.

Civilian Civil Defense teams,
Bomb shelters,
Talking John Birch Society paranoia,
Divorce, alcoholism,

Cowboys and Indians,
The CIA, the Cold War, Communists, the Axis
of Evil,
another war, global terror, an out of control
right wing government.

★★★

Speaker One: Narrator

Bud wrote about his father and his father's secret life as a CIA agent. My father led a semi-secret life as a person who drank too much. His life, perhaps like Bud's father's life, segues into this question: "What went wrong with our generation's and our parents' generation's version of the American Dream?" And like in George Clooney's 2005 movie *Good Night, and Good Luck*, good luck was no longer enough, even if Mamie Eisenhower did wear bangs, just like my grandmother, and even if my father and his Civilian Defense Team kept the United States safe from the Communists.

Scene Eight: Back to the Beginning

Speaker One: Narrator

Today I want to write my way out of this history, and this is why I write this mystory, my version of autoethnography. I want to push back, intervene, be vulnerable, tell another story; I want to contest what happened.

(Pelias, 2011, p. 12)

★★★

I want to return to the memories of my childhood, that last Sunday when my family visited the Mesquaki Reservation. We were happy that day. Alcoholism had not yet hit our little house, but A.A. was not far off. As a family we were slipping. A day on the reservation brought escape from what was coming. Could things have happened differently if my father had stopped drinking on that day? I know my brother and I fought. Could my father and mother have recovered a love that day that would have withstood infidelities and drunkenness? Did Indians have anything at all to do with this? Maybe an alternative ending is fruitless. Why even try? No more cowboys and Indians. No more Lone Ranger and Tonto performances.

★★★

Speaker Two: Narrator as Guy Maddin

I think I'm like the narrator in Guy Maddin's 2007 film, *My Winnipeg*.[8] In the film Maddin returns to his family home and rents the house for a month so he can re-do some things that happened in that house when he was 12 years old. He hires actors to play his mother, father, brother, and sister. He rents a pet dog.[9] When the month is up, there are still issues that have not been resolved.

★★★

Speaker One: Narrator as Self

I could be like Gay Maddin. I'd rent the Iowa farmhouse for one week, the house where Dad and Shirley danced too close, and I'd have mom tell Shirley to take her hands off of her husband. Or maybe I'd go back to the little house on Coralville and have Dad and Mom pretend that they didn't have to be drinking in order to act as if they loved each other.

Scene Nine: Kent Monkman[10] and Karl May[11]

Curtain rises.

The German band the Johnny Ca$H Brothers quietly plays cowboy music.

Speaker One: Author as Narrator

Let's try one more time to get out of this mess. Maybe Kent Monkman, the radical Cree painter, can help me get past this impasse of forever playing Indian. In his current exhibition, which he calls "The Atelier" (workshop), Kent challenges the Lone Ranger–Tonto narrative. He has a winged male nude pose next to an easel. Through the studio window the viewer can see a two-panel installation: "Tonto & the Lone Ranger," and "Winnetou & Shatterhand." In each painting the white man—Shatterhand, Lone Ranger—lounges on lush verdant grass in front of a roaring waterfall. The two Indians—Tonto and Winnetou—stand in front and above the White men. Winnetou faces the waterfalls while Tonto has his back turned to the falls, facing the Lone Ranger, as if giving him directions.

Speaker Two: Narrator Number Two

Monkman turns the tables. Neither Tonto nor Winnetou is the White man's trusty sidekick. He makes the White man the sidekick. Tonto has gained the upper hand, just as Old Shatterhand is subservient to Winnetou. Monkman creates an alternative Native American heritage.

(http://www.pfoac.com/assets/KM/images/Miss_america/
KM_2012_W&ST&TLR_large.jpg)

Speaker One: Narrator to Self

Would I have wanted to play Tonto if the Lone Ranger was my sidekick? Maybe we can stop constructing these stories, but probably not in the near future.[12] It is like a never-ending minstrel show, as if Whites are not able to let go of the myth that says "we are superior" to all non-White persons.

Speaker One: Tonto

I'm not optimistic of any letting go. Do you know about the Lone Ranger and Tonto jokes? This one appeared in the January 17–23, 2013, edition of the Champaign, Illinois, *News-Gazette* (p. 16):

★★★

Lone Ranger and Tonto Joke

The Lone Ranger and Tonto were at the bar drinking, when in walks a cowboy who yells, "Whose white horse it that outside?"

The Lone Ranger finishes off his whiskey, slams down the glass, turns around, and says, "It's my horse. Why do you want to know?"

The cowboy looks at him and says, "Well, your horse is standing out there in the sun and he don't look too good."

The Lone Ranger and Tonto run outside, and they see that Silver is in bad shape, suffering from heat exhaustion.

The Lone Ranger moves his horse into the shade and gets a bucket of water. He then pours some of the water over the horse and gives the rest to Silver to drink. It is then he notices that there isn't a breeze so he asks Tonto if he would start running around Silver to get some air flowing and perhaps cool him down.

Being a faithful friend, Tonto starts running around Silver. The Lone Ranger stands there for a bit then realizes there is not much more he can do, so he goes back into the bar and orders another whiskey.

After a bit a cowboy walks in and says, "Who's white horse is that outside?"

Slowly the Lone Ranger turns around and says, "That is my horse, what is wrong with him now?"

"Nothing," replies the cowboy, "I just wanted to let you know that you left your Injun running."

★★★

Scene Ten: Dancing Indians

The Johnny Ca$H Brothers are playing cowboy music:

Speaker One: Narrator as Observer
(Denzin, 2008, pp. 26–28)

August 3, 1998: A blue, wind-swept Montana night, a red sun setting over the Beartooth Mountains. It's hot inside the crowded Red Lodge Civic Auditorium. "Montana Night," a special part of this year's Festival of Nations Celebration, is about to begin. The lights dim. The mistress of ceremonies asks the audience to "Give a Big Red Lodge welcome to Crow Indian Chief Haywood Big Day and his family, who are visitors tonight from the Crow Reservation near Pryor." In full tribal regalia, Chief Big Day walks to the center of the stage. I flash back to those "Cowboy and Indian" television shows of my childhood. The chief looks like a television Indian. Maybe he is another version of "Kaw-Liga," the drugstore wooden Indian in the Hank Williams's song—the sad Indian who never smiled at the little Indian maiden next door. The chief, now acting like the Lone Ranger's Tonto, beckons to his family. In full ceremonial regalia, his wife and daughter solemnly walk across the floor and stand behind him. Wearing Los Angeles Lakers basketball jerseys, his four young grandsons follow their mother to the center of the gym. The chief announces, "We are First Nation. We will do a War Dance." Seven Indians, four dressed in L.A. Lakers look-alike jerseys, do a war dance, heads bowed, arms moving up and down, across the gym floor.

★★★

The crowd of over 800 stands as one, applauding Chief Big Day and his family, chanting "First Nation, First Nation." I can hear Paul Revere and the Raiders: "They took the whole Cherokee Nation and put us on the reservation."[13]

A postmodern racial performance right here in Red Lodge, Montana.

Scene Eleven: The Sting of Memory

Speaker One: Narrator to Audience

June 2, 1953: Family photo, 403 West 3rd Street, Indianola, Iowa. We stand in a group, looking western in western cloths: father, hand on hip, cowboy hat, cowboy boots, wide silver belt; mother, cowgirl hat, red bandana around her neck, wide silver belt; Mark, my brother, and me, Norman, wearing little cowboy outfits—hats, vests, cowboy boots, toy pistols in leather holsters. Forced smiles, we have slightly down-cast, but far-off looks in our eyes. Our family is about to fall apart, and everybody knows it.

★★★

July 5, 1955: In my memory I return to our little house on Third Avenue in Indianola, Iowa. Father has returned from a fishing trip in Ontario,

Canada. He has a cowboy hat pushed back in his head. Mother greets him at the door. Father is drunk. He hands mother a Hudson's Bay wool blanket as a present and promptly leaves for the office. I still have that blanket.

Speaker Two: Narrator

I want to return to 1955 and start my family story all over. What if father had returned home sober? Can I go back to before June 2, 1953? Is there no going back?

Coda Number Three

Curtain rises. Spotlight shines on solitary speaker, center stage. The sounds of Dave Brubeck's quartet playing "Take Five" can still be heard.

Speaker One: Sandra Goodall

There is no good way to break this news, but we wanted to let people know as soon as possible. Bud passed away early this morning (Friday, August 24, 2012: 15:10).

Speaker Two: Bud Goodall

As for my name, I'll always be called Bud. I'm full-grown now.

Speaker One: Narrator

I'll double-back here. In *A Need to Know*, Bud writes his father's life story through the 1950 Cold War. I've written portions of my father's life story through the same war, but added Indians and alcoholism.

Bud writes:

Speaker Two: Bud

I thought I had freed myself from my mother and father's life story, but I had not, and they both earned a better narrative ending than the one I had previously given them.

Speaker One: Narrator

And so it is for me. My father and mother deserved better. But here at the end Bud's gift shines through. He has given me, he has given each of us, the narrative tools to tell the stories we need to tell. Rest in peace Bud. What we have inherited from your narrative tells us that there is still a lot of work to do.

THE END

Notes

1 This essay re-works materials in Denzin (2008, 2011, 2013a, 2013b).
2 See also Goodall, 2009.
3 *Karl* Friedrich *May* (1842–1912) was a popular German writer, famous for adventure novels set in the American Old West. The Karl May Festival began in 1952, in a natural outdoor amphitheater created in the side of the town's chalk mountain. Officials of the Third Reich used the site as a gathering place for political events. The festival productions feature German, Czech, Polish, French, Turkish, Italian, American, Swedish, Spanish, Japanese, Navajo, and Apache performers. The Karl May Museum was founded in 1928 by Klara May (May's second wife) and Patty Frank, a former stable hand for Buffalo Bill's Wild West show. May's museum became a meeting place for German Indian hobbyists who dressed as cowboys and Indians, hosted real Indians and Cowboys from visiting Wild West shows, and held memorial talks on May's grave (Warren, 2005). The first German Cowboy Club was founded in 1913 in Munich. The German hobbyists had American counterparts as Boy Scouts and Seton's Woodcraft Indians (Warren, 2005).
4 My father's mother's family came from Brandenburg, Germany, in 1883.
5 This is a play on Churchill's (1994) *Indians Are Us? Culture and Genocide in Native North America*.
6 The oldest festival in Germany and the most famous passion play that is still performed today. It reenacts the suffering and crucifixion of Christ as a form of devotion.
7 This paragraph steals from Burke (2009).
8 Maddin is a well-known Canadian filmmaker. *My Winnipeg* was awarded the prize for Best Canadian Feature Film at the 2007 Toronto International Film Festival.
9 His pet dog died. His sister had a big fight with his mother. His father may have died.
10 Kent Monkman (b. 1965) is a Canadian First Nations artist of Cree and Irish ancestry (see http://kentmonkman.com/main.php).
11 May's novels featured an Apache warrior named Winnetou and his sidekick, a German engineer named Old Shatterhand.
12 In 2013, Walt Disney Pictures released a remake of *The Lone Ranger*, starring Johnny Depp as Tonto and a cast of Hollywood A-listers. With a $225 million budget, the big-screen treatment was the first theatrical film to feature the Lone Ranger and Tonto characters since 1981.
13 A rock-and-roll group from the 1970s. I thank C. Michael Elavsky and Robert Sloane for these lines and information.

References

Amira de la Garza, S., Krizek, R., & Trujillo, N. (Eds.) (2012). *Celebrating Bud. A festschrift honoring the life and work of H. L. 'Bud' Goodall, Jr.* Tempe, AZ: Innovative Inquiry.

Benjamin, W. (1969). *Illuminations* (H. Zohn, Trans.). New York: Harcourt, Brace & World.

Burke, J. L. (2009). *Rain gods*. New York: Simon & Schuster.

Churchill, W. (1994). *Indians are us? Culture and genocide in native North America*. Monroe, ME: Common Courage Press.

Denzin, N. K. (2013a). *Indians on display: Global commodification of native America in performance, art, and museums*. Walnut Creek, CA: Left Coast Press.

Denzin, N K. (2013b). Interpretive autoethnography. In S. H. Jones, T. Adams, & C. Ellis (Eds.), *Handbook of autoethnography* (pp. 23–39). Walnut Creek, CA: Left Coast Press.

Denzin, N. K. (2011). *Custer on canvas: Representing Indians, memory, and violence in the New West*. Walnut Creek, CA: Left Coast Press.

Denzin, N. K. (2008). *Searching for Yellowstone: Race, gender, family and memory in the postmodern West*. Walnut Creek, CA: Left Coast Press.

Goodall, H. L. (2009, Spring). Between the bookends: Review of Norman K. Denzin, *Searching for Yellowstone: Race, gender, family and memory in the postmodern West. Points West,* p. 30.

Goodall, H. L. (Bud), Jr. (2008a). *A need to know: The clandestine history of a CIA family.* Walnut Creek, CA: Left Coast Press.

Goodall, H. L. (Bud), Jr. (2008b). *Writing qualitative inquiry: Self, stories, and academic life.* Walnut Creek, CA: Left Coast Press.

Goodall, H. L. (Bud), Jr. (2000). *Writing the new ethnography.* Walnut Creek, CA: AltiMira.

Gruber, R. E. (2004, August 7). European festivals keep wild west alive and kickin'. *New York Times.* Retrieved from http://www.nytimes.com/2004/08/07/style/07iht-trfest_ed3_.html.

Lopinto, N. (2009, May–June). Der Indianer: Why do 40,000 Germans spend their weekends dressed as Native Americans? *Utne Reader.* Retrieved from http://www.utne.com/mind-and-body/germans-weekends-native-americans-indian-culture.aspx.

Pelias, R. J. (2011). Writing into position. In N. K. Denzin & Y. S. Lincoln (Eds.), *Handbook of qualitative research* (4th ed., pp. 659–668). Thousand Oaks, CA: SAGE.

Ulmer, G. (1989). *Teletheory.* New York: Routledge.

Warren, L. S. (2005). *Buffalo Bill's America: William Cody and the Wild West Show.* New York: Alfred A. Knopf.

CONTRIBUTORS

Editor Bios

Norman K. Denzin is Distinguished Professor of Communications, College of Communications Scholar, and Research Professor of Communications, Sociology, and Humanities at the University of Illinois, Urbana–Champaign. One of the world's foremost authorities on qualitative research and cultural criticism, Denzin is the author or editor of more than two dozen books, including *The Qualitative Manifesto*; *Qualitative Inquiry Under Fire*; *Reading Race*; *Interpretive Ethnography*; *The Cinematic Society*; *The Voyeur's Gaze*; *The Alcoholic Self*; and a trilogy on the American West. He is past editor of *The Sociological Quarterly*, co-editor (with Yvonna S. Lincoln) of four editions of the landmark *Handbook of Qualitative Research*, co-editor (with Michael D. Giardina) of 11 plenary volumes from the annual International Congress of Qualitative Inquiry, co-editor (with Giardina) of *Qualitative Inquiry—Past, Present, & Future: A Critical Reader*, co-editor (with Lincoln) of the methods journal *Qualitative Inquiry*, founding editor of *Cultural Studies ⇔ Critical Methodologies* and *International Review of Qualitative Research*, editor of three book series, and founding director of the International Congress of Qualitative Inquiry.

Michael D. Giardina is Associate Professor of Sport, Culture, and Politics and Associate Director of the Center for Sport, Health, and Equitable Development at Florida State University. He is the author of *Sport, Spectacle, and NASCAR Nation: Consumption and the Cultural Politics of Neoliberalism* (Palgrave, 2011, with Joshua Newman)—which received the 2012 Outstanding Book Award from the North American Society for the Sociology of Sport (NASSS) and was named to the 2012 *CHOICE* "Outstanding Academic Titles" list—and *Sporting Pedagogies: Performing Culture & Identity in the Global Arena* (Peter Lang, 2005), which received the 2006

Outstanding Book Award from NASSS. He is also the editor or co-editor of more than a dozen books on qualitative inquiry, cultural studies, and interpretive research, including most recently *Qualitative Inquiry—Past, Present, & Future: A Critical Reader* (with Norman K. Denzin; Left Coast Press, 2015). He is editor of the *Sociology of Sport Journal*, special issues editor of *Cultural Studies ⟺ Critical Methodologies*, and the Associate Director of the International Congress of Qualitative Inquiry.

Author Bios

Tony E. Adams is Associate Professor and Chair of the Department of Communication, Media, and Theatre at Northeastern Illinois University. His first book, *Narrating the Closet: An Autoethnography of Same Sex Desire* (Left Coast Press, 2011), received three national book awards, and the *Handbook of Autoethnography* (Left Coast Press, 2013), a collection he co-edited with Stacy Holman Jones and Carolyn Ellis, received the "Best Edited Book Award" from the Ethnography Division of the National Communication Association. Most recently, he co-edited, with Jonathan Wyatt, *On (Writing) Families: Autoethnographies of Presence and Absence, Love and Loss* (Sense Publishers, 2014), and co-authored, with Carolyn Ellis and Stacy Holman Jones, *Autoethnography* (Oxford University Press, 2015).

Robin M. Boylorn is Associate Professor of Communication and Information Sciences at the University of Alabama. She is the author of *Sweetwater: Black Women and Narratives of Resilience* (Peter Lang, 2012) and co-editor, with Mark P. Orbe, of *Critical Autoethnography: Writing Cultural Identity in Everyday Life* (Left Coast Press, 2013). Her work has also appeared in journals such as *Qualitative Inquiry*, *Cultural Studies ⟺ Critical Methodologies*, *International Review of Qualitative Research*, and *Critical Studies in Media Communication*. She is also a member of the scholar-activist group, the Crunk Feminist Collective.

Kathy Charmaz is Professor of Sociology and Director of the Faculty Writing Program at Sonoma State University. She has written, co-authored, or co-edited more than a dozen books including *Good Days, Bad Days: The Self in Chronic Illness and Time*, which won awards from the Pacific Sociological Association and the Society for the Study of Symbolic Interaction, and *Constructing Grounded Theory*, which received a Critics' Choice Award from the American Educational Studies Association. She has also served as President of the Pacific Sociological Association; President and Vice-President of the Society for the Study of Symbolic Interaction; Vice-President of Alpha Kappa Delta, the international honorary for sociology; editor of *Symbolic Interaction*; and Chair of the Medical Sociology Section of the American Sociological Association. She received the 2001 Feminist Mentors Award and the 2006 George Herbert Mead award for lifetime achievement from the Society for the Study of Symbolic Interaction.

Bronwyn Davies is an Independent Scholar and Professorial Fellow at the University of Melbourne, Australia. She is the author of more than 130 book chapters and articles, as well as 17 books, including *Listening to Children: Being and Becoming* (Routledge, 2014), *Deleuze and Collaborative Writing* (with Jonathan Wyatt, Ken Gale, and Susanne Gannon; Peter Lang, 2011), and *Frogs and Snails and Feminist Tales* (Hampton, 2003), which has been translated in Swedish, German, and Spanish.

Valerie J. Janesick is Professor of Educational Leadership and Policy Studies, University of South Florida. She is the author of numerous books on qualitative inquiry, including *"Stretching" Exercises for Qualitative Research* (Sage, 2015; now in its fourth edition), *Contemplative Qualitative Inquiry: Practicing the Zen of Research* (Left Coast Press, 2015), and *Oral History for the Qualitative Researcher: Choreographing the Story* (Guilford, 2010).

Mirka Koro-Ljungberg is Professor of Qualitative Research at Arizona State University. Her scholarship operates in the intersection of methodology, philosophy, and socio-cultural critique, and her work aims to contribute to methodological knowledge, experimentation, and theoretical development across various traditions associated with qualitative research. She is the author of *Reconceptualizing Qualitative Research: Methodologies Without Methodology* (Sage, 2015).

Margaret Kovach is Associate Professor of Educational Foundations & Educational Administration at the University of Saskatchewan, Canada. She is the author of *Indigenous Methodologies: Characteristics, Conversations, and Contexts* (University of Toronto Press, 2009), which in 2010 received the Saskatchewan Book Award for Scholarly Writing. She is also the inaugural recipient of the 2010 University of Saskatchewan Provost Award for Excellence in Aboriginal Education. Her work has appeared in journals such as *Canadian Journal of Native Education*, *First People Child and Family Review*, and *Critical Social Work Journal*.

Patricia Leavy is an Independent Scholar (formerly Associate Professor of Sociology, Chair of Sociology & Criminology, and Founding Director of Gender Studies at Stonehill College). Her 19 published books include *Method Meets Art: Arts-Based Research Practice* (first and second editions, Guilford), *The Oxford Handbook of Qualitative Research* (Oxford University Press), *Fiction as Research Practice* (Left Coast Press), and the best-selling novels *Blue*, *Low-Fat Love*, and *American Circumstance* (all with Sense Publishers). She has received numerous awards including the New England Sociological Association 2010 New England Sociologist of the Year Award, the American Creativity Association 2014 Special Achievement Award, the American Educational Research Association Qualitative SIG 2015 Egon Guba Memorial Keynote Lecture Award, and the International Congress of Qualitative Inquiry 2015 Special Career Award.

Elizabeth Adams St. Pierre is Professor and Graduate Coordinator of Language and Literacy Education at the University of Georgia. Her work has appeared in a range of scholarly journals, including *International Review of Qualitative Research*, *Educational Researcher*, *Qualitative Inquiry*, *Journal of Contemporary Ethnography*, and *International Journal of Qualitative Studies in Education*. She is also the editor of *Working the Ruins: Feminist Poststructural Theory and Methods in Education* (Routledge, 2000; with Wanda Pillow).

Sophie Tamas is Assistant Professor in the School of Canadian Studies at Carleton University, Canada. She is the author of *Life After Leaving: The Remains of Spousal Abuse* (Left Coast Press, 2011). She has held a SSHRC postdoctoral fellowship in Emotional Geography at Queen's University and was named a Banting Fellow in 2012–2013. Her work has appeared in journals such as *Emotion, Space, and Society*, *Cultural Studies ⇔ Critical Methodologies*, and *Qualitative Inquiry*.

Jasmine B. Ulmer is Assistant Professor and Qualitative Research Program Director at Wayne State University. In addition to critical qualitative inquiry, her research interests include visual methodologies, digital methodologies, and writing qualitative inquiry. Her publications include articles in *Qualitative Inquiry*, *Educational Philosophy and Theory*, *Research in Dance Education*, and *Discourse: Studies in the Cultural Politics of Education*.

INDEX